# Writer on the Side: How to Write Your Book Around Your 9 to 5 Job

Bryan Cohen

# LEGAL PAGE

# DEDICATION

I dedicate this book to all of the cubicle workers out there who have dared to dream about becoming writers on the side.

# CONTENTS

# INTRODUCTION

I spoke with a friend a few weeks ago. I won't name names, but I had the fortune of travelling with her and about 20 other members of my English Department classmates to Oxford, England during one college summer. The subject of our journey across the ocean was Shakespeare, one of the most prolific writers ever. One sunny day (and it was particularly sunny that summer in England, thankfully) we all sat in a graveyard at the University and took turns reading all of Shakespeare's 154 sonnets. We also saw or read many of his 37 plays. The trip was enlightening and I am certain that it inspired me in part to be an actor and a writer.

When I spoke with my friend recently, the subject of book titling came up as I was attempting to figure out the title for my second book, a collection of essays. She presented me with a title idea for her own book, which I won't write here for fear of it being stolen. It was fantastic and it perfectly fit her personality and writing style. She then stuck a giant spike into the side of her circus tent of an idea, deflating it and sending it crashing to the ground.

"Of course, I've titled ten thousand books that will never get written."

At first, the motivational writer in me wanted to say hundreds of different pieces of advice that would lift her up and make her want to start writing her fantastically titled book. After a few tidbits of wisdom slipped out, I realized to myself that I had once thought the same thing.

I once believed that I would never be a real writer. I believed I would never publish or self-publish something that other people would care about. Something changed for me, and I'll get into that a little bit later in the book, especially in the "My Story" section in Chapter 1.

## Life Lasts a Long Time

Here is the thing about becoming an author. Some people, beyond all odds, if they have the ability to write, will become writers much, much later in life. They may have had another career for several decades of their lives. They may have been a housewife or househusband taking care of their families well into arthritis, heart-healthy diets and becoming grandparents. They may have even been part of a traumatic experience or two that made them believe they couldn't do anything anymore, let alone write a book that people would read.

There are countless stories of these supposed late bloomers in the history of English writing. Anthony Burgess, famous for his book *A Clockwork Orange* did not publish his first novel until the age of 39. Joseph Conrad didn't even know English until he was around 21 years old, but after writing in the language around the age of 32, he was still able to publish such great works as *Heart of Darkness* after the age of 37. Author Laura Ingalls Wilder become a newspaper columnist in her forties, but did not begin publishing her novels until her sixties, with the *Little House on the Prairie* series.

How many of these people do you think had to push back internal and external criticism along the lines of "you'll never get this done" or "you're not a writer, you've been doing something else your entire life"? Personally, I've dealt with internal doubting that felt heavy enough to knock over an elephant. When I left college, I struggled with depression and a lack of personal meaning. I was working a 9 to 5 job doing data entry while I took some improvisational comedy classes. The classes were great, but between a large commute and feeling soullessly empty during the job, I remember thinking to myself, "You're wasting your life!" I was 22, and I already thought I was done for. How's that for dramatic?

But that's the thing. We hear all these stories of child prodigies and authors like Stephen King who are so prolific, who write so much, that we assume if we haven't started yet, we'll never get to the finish line.

We need to start choosing our comparisons better. If we're going to compare ourselves to someone we should compare ourselves to authors like Laura Ingalls Wilder or Anthony Burgess, who had no writing published at all until they were close to or past the age of 40.

The real trick though, is to realize that writing a book is not a race. It's more like a journey of self-discovery. It's like climbing a mountain alone that nobody has ever climbed before. There is no "fastest time" award or anything like that. You are climbing that mountain and there is no comparison at all. If you take two months or 20 years, you will still be in first place because nobody has written *your* book, nobody has climbed *your* mountain.

## But I'm Too Busy

Many of you will read the above and your response will be, "you're full of crap!" I completely understand this reaction because it took me several years of reading and listening to what I "needed to hear" to become an author and to get motivated to write before I truly believed it. For you wonderful people, who need a truck to hit you to make you realize you might not be headed in the right direction, just read on and hopefully you'll see the headlights bearing down.

*Some of you* will have a different reaction. You will acknowledge that you do want to write. You want to be like these "late bloomers" (or "early bloomers" depending on how old you are when you read this) who have gotten something published or self-published. You want to be an author! Your response to this desire, however, is something along the lines of "But, I'm too busy!"

Not to sound too much like a salesman, but "this is the book for you!" (cue infomercial audience applause)

At least, this book was written for you, the few, the proud, the people who want to be authors but like most of the world have jobs that either run from 9 to 5 or that generally take up 40 or more hours in your week.

I'm here to tell you that it is possible to become an author despite most of your time being taken up by working and sleeping. Even if you have a family and you spend your additional free time taking care of your kids, your spouse and your bills, it is possible to become an author. Now, obviously, the less time you have, the longer it will take, but you still have a shot to get that book that's been bouncing around your head onto the page.

Some of you chosen few will respond like the earlier group with the phrase, "You're full of crap!" Which is perfectly fine; I have developed a thick skin to such silly, non-specific criticism. Those of you who are still on board might ask the productive question of, "What do I need to make this happen?"

The three things you need are desire, time and tools.

Desire is simple and complicated at the same time. Desire means that you want to do this and that you're willing to push past all of your fear and obstacles to make it happen. The fear and obstacles are what make desire complex, because many people will succumb to these road blocks and never achieve their loftier lifetime goals. Getting to the level of desire necessary to write a book will be covered in Chapter 2 called "Wanting It."

By time required for writing, I'm not referring to eight hours a day and I may not even be referring to eight hours a week. I simply mean that you are willing to put aside a little bit of time, perhaps even 15 minutes a day toward straight up writing. If you are constantly overwhelmed and you are hard pressed to find any time for yourself, than you are in need of our third important item.

Tools are tricks that either create more time for yourself or help you to generate ideas for your writing while you are otherwise busy. Most of this book is dedicated toward using tools to either generate writing time or to brainstorm about writing while you're doing other things. There are chapters in the book devoted to the morning, afternoon, evening and the weekends and they are full of tools you can use to get you into author mode.

And here's the best thing about these tools. You don't need to use them all. In fact, you may only need to use one or two.

I have taken a kitchen sink approach with the tools sections, giving you every idea I've ever used or ever thought of that could help you to use your time more effectively. While I have used most of the ideas in the book, it's rare that I am using all of them at the same time. Using just a few of the tools occasionally has generated enough ideas and writing time to help me to finish this, which is my fourth book.

Some of the tools you will like and some of them you won't like (or they won't be possible for you in your line of work). Take the ones you can use and apply them immediately.

Before long, you will find that with just a few tweaks here and there, you can add a new title to the way you describe yourself, "And I'm a writer on the side."

## Final Thoughts

There is no telling what this book will cause you to do. You may smile, you may frown and you may read it cover to cover until the words are indelibly scrawled into your memory.

But if you don't actually do any of the suggestions within its pages, you will probably not have a lot of luck as an author.

This is a book full of tips and tricks that can get you writing despite having most of your hours taken up by "the man" during your week. You need to actually perform some of the tips and tricks to get some benefit out of it. Too often, I see people who will listen to an audio tape and read a new book about improving their lives. Then, they read another book and listen to another tape. And so on and so forth.

But they never *do* anything that the book tells them.

I've been guilty of this, I admit to it. I'm here to tell you that it's a waste of time to just read the book and hope that the motivation within will be absorbed through that thick skull of yours. If I suggest that you eat a healthier, higher energy breakfast … I want you to try it! If I suggest that you keep a notepad near your desk so that you can jot down writing ideas … I want you to try it! If I suggest you set up a writing area for yourself somewhere in your apartment or house, I damn well expect you to give it a shot!

Please, please, please, try at least one of the things in this book. Hell, get a friend at work in a similar boat to do the same thing. Push each other to take some action. Whatever you need to do to get your motor running, make it so!

While my second desire is that you enjoy the book, my first is that it helps you to improve your life and your creativity and to achieve your writing goals.

If you find yourself stuck, please wander over to my Build Creative Writing Ideas website and shoot me a message. I'm always willing to help, if there's something the book doesn't cover in enough detail.

I wish you good luck, great skill and the best motivation possible.

Happy writing!

Sincerely,
Bryan Cohen
Author of *Writer on the Side*

# 1 MY STORY

## The Post-College Blues

I was afraid. I had just graduated from college and I was absolutely terrified of becoming a part of the real world. Throughout most of school, I had actually been somewhat focused, producing and directing some theatre, writing stories for my creative writing classes, and getting the full college experience with parties, girlfriends and activities. During my junior year, after a few dating relationships went sour, I had thrown myself into my work and considered myself a full-time actor and writer, writing my first full play in my dorm's laundry room with a second play that I had co-written going up that summer.

By my senior year, however, I had a full blown case of senior-itis. I had stopped working as hard and moved my work and my development far down my list of priorities. While many people were securing jobs for the following year, I was putting off the inevitable. I even decided to stick around Chapel Hill for the whole summer, working for the University to fix up dorm rooms for the following year. It was obvious that I was grabbing hold of college and that someone or something was going to have to drag me kicking and screaming away from it.

After a summer filled with drama in my personal life, I finally ended up in the suburbs of Chicago. I decided that I was an improvisational comedian, partly because it was a lot of fun, but I think a little bit because it was an artistic career choice with little to no commitment necessary.

I took on 9 to 5 temp jobs, because they similarly offered little commitment. On days that I had comedy classes or rehearsal, I would commute into the city, have some laughs with friends and colleagues and then make the long commute home. While this put me on trains over two hours a day, I hardly took a second to think about anything productive. I spent my time focusing on past dating relationships, regret at not doing as much as I wanted to creatively and plenty of sad sack wallowing. On days without comedy class, the amount of wallowing time doubled.

I remember looking at myself in the mirror one day thinking, "You have all this time, why aren't you doing anything with it?" I was stuck in neutral (or maybe even reverse). I couldn't start anything, or at least, I wouldn't start anything. Partly it was fear of failure. Also, it was partly fear of success, believing at least in part that I wasn't worth it. Over the course of my first three years in Chicago (which eventually took me into the city itself) I feel like I packed in over a decade of worrying and negativity.

## A Turning Point

I bounced from temp job to temp job, eventually settling on a job at a coffee shop, which gave me a bit more time per week to find acting gigs and work on any shows I could get up the will to produce. The coffee shop gig was a bit less money per week, and I was already hurting financially, so this caused me to get into a mess with my credit cards. In a drastic effort to turn things around, I attempted to produce a Web series, borrowing tons of money from my relatives, friends, and various loan websites. Instead of taking the slow and steady approach, I thought I could do it all in one fell swoop.

It failed. Now, I had hit the bottom.

Here's the great thing about the bottom though. You can either look at the ground the rest of your life, or you can take the opportunity to look up at all the other directions that you can go. Thankfully, I chose this second path and I started looking for a way to dig myself out of this hole.

On a random Internet search, I came upon the subject of "Personal Development." I didn't really know what this was, and I certainly felt "underdeveloped personally" so I figured I'd give it a shot. The subject was a lot more multi-faceted than it appeared at first glance. It dealt with subjects like optimism (which I was certainly lacking), creating goals and a plan for yourself (ditto) and attracting positive situations and people into your life (which I needed desperately).

I threw myself into the personal development game. I would listen to podcasts I found online, I made a popular personal development site into my home page and I started talking about it to everybody I knew. I noticed that some of the extremely negative people in my life, started to fade out and that my financial situation somewhat stabilized while I concentrated on the positivity of this new subject matter.

I wanted to do something with the energy and motivation I gained from all my research and excitement. I had read in Stephen Covey's *7 Habits of Highly Effective People* that you learn 90% of what you teach, so I created a website dedicated to teaching people how to push past their blocks and start writing immediately. The site was called Build Creative Writing Ideas. It was the jumping off point for over a hundred articles and the several books that I've written. Even in just the first few months, I received some amazing comments from people who read my work and gained some sort of hope from it all. While this didn't correct my course completely, I felt like I was finally starting to head in the right direction.

## Barista to Freelancer to Author

Despite gaining some ground on feeling more purposeful, I was still a barista at a coffee shop and I was still paying off some pretty hefty bills. During a free trip to Israel through the Taglit Birthright program, I had a moment of clarity. This moment caused me to put in my two week notice upon my return. The problem was, I still didn't have a plan, but I figured I'd leave it to chance and try to find something more in my wheelhouse than coffee and pastries.

While I took on various gigs like promotional work and acting, the one I settled on as the direction I was supposed to go in was freelance writing. Most of my work was in the form of articles for various websites and it paid by the article. While it wasn't a 9 to 5 job, to ensure that I was moving upward financially, I usually worked over 40 hours a week. It was very cool to be writing for most if not all of my income from week to week, but I was getting drained. Plus, I hardly ever had time to work on my Build Creative Writing Ideas website. And when I did have time, I felt creatively stifled from writing all the dang time!

The solution I found was to find something I could write quickly and easily on the side for BCWI while I still made my living through writing articles. I started writing pages on my site dedicated toward writing prompts (also known as story starters). I would come up with a particular topic and generate 10 ideas per page that people could use to get their thoughts out of their heads and onto the page. I had previously done a few in the early days of the site and they ended up being the most popular by far.

Within a year, I had over 75 pages of prompts (a bit over 750 prompts in total) and I was almost completely burned out from my 40 hours a week of article writing. I took on a few less taxing freelance jobs and some extra promotional work, but I was still having trouble making ends meet.

Another random online search took me to a page about an eBook writer who was having major success without getting something published the old fashioned way. An idea dawned on me.

"750 prompts are pretty close to 1,000. 1,000 prompts would be an awesome book."

I had an idea. I had the desire and I had the need. At that point, I had also developed lots of little tips and tricks to get myself writing these prompts on the side in the first place. With my newfound goal in mind, I had little to no problem finishing the 1,000. I self-published the book under the title *1,000 Creative Writing Prompts: Ideas for Blogs, Scripts,*

*Stories and More.* I put the book up on my website and later on the sites Amazon Kindle and Smashwords.

The book started selling well enough for me to determine the experiment a success. While I was still doing some freelance and promotional work, I was a published author. I had gone from a barista at the bottom to an author … somewhat at the middle. I kept writing books on the side and here I am working on my fourth book.

## What I Learned

When I pulled myself out of the emotional muck and stepped back from everything a bit, I was truly able to see the many ways in which I'd been holding myself back. I didn't need to work fewer hours or empty my schedule entirely (especially since writing all week long just burned me out more). I needed to work more efficiently and positively with the time I had. I didn't become a real writer until I worked around 40 hours a week on my income and made efforts to create what I wanted to write on the side.

I didn't become a published author until I had a clear goal in mind and some tips and tricks in my repertoire to use during my spare time.

Since, like I said, you learn about 90% of what you teach, I want to spread these tips and tricks for writing and motivation to all of you. I want you to believe that you can both come up with ten thousand titles and write them as well (perhaps, a few less than ten thousand, but still). Writing something on the side, like a night school education, takes a bit longer than a full-time writing career, but it can still be extremely rewarding.

Most of this book is dedicated to the tools you can use during the morning, afternoon, evening and weekend to improve your motivation and to put pen to paper.

What everything starts with, however, is a goal. A clear idea of what you want to accomplish with your writing. It's this "wanting it" that acts as the spark to cause everything to combust (in a starting-your-engine kind of way). If you think you're ready to take the first step in the "Writer on the Side" process, please continue on to the next chapter.

# 2 WANTING IT

I want to preface this chapter by saying that there are a lot of wonderful books and audio programs available about setting goals and making them an important part of your life. I should know, I've read them all (or at least some). From the books, I've picked up a lot of fantastic ideas and I've also found a lot of things that didn't work for me. Regardless, I will tell you some of the ideas I've learned and I will tell you the exact formula that worked for me. I will try to give you a great deal of options so that you can pick and choose like a buffet until you find the right combo platter for you. Deal? Deal!

## Picking Your Goal

Most people have but a few goals in their lives. One of the major ones tends to be something like this: "I want to get through every horrible, boring day until I can get home and then zone out in front of my phone or television until the next day starts." There are more than a few flaws to this goal. Other than the fact that it's not positive, it doesn't have any direction and it never changes, there is a huge issue with it that is both sad and true.

It is more or less the default setting for most people with a 9 to 5 job.

This is the tough trait of goals that people don't realize. If you don't pick a goal, your brain essentially picks it for you. The brain loves habits whether they are good or bad. If you come home every day and watch television, your brain is going to start expecting that, to the point that if you skip it for a day, you start missing it. Pushing this habit on yourself has made television-watching a subconscious goal for you. This is similar to a bowl of ice cream every night before bed, five hours of checking your e-mail and Facebook each day or going out to the bars for a bender every weekend.

People will then assume that this habit they have *trained* themselves to do, is a part of who they are. They say things like "I'm just angry in the morning, that's just who I am," or "How could I give up (this food) or (that drink), it's my favorite and I just love it too much," or "I'll never write a book, I can't work it into my schedule."

Here's the flip side of the coin though. Since you can choose your goals, if you do decide to actually pick something, you can choose any goal that you want. Let's say you currently watch television three hours per night. If you made the decision that you no longer wanted to make television your goal and that becoming an author was your new goal, this is a somewhat simple shift.

I'm not saying that you could immediately go from watching television to becoming Stephen King, but even that simple shift will have you headed in the right direction. The reason it isn't easy at first is because you are trained to watch television, you're trained to eat that ice cream and you are trained *against* being a writer.

But just like your parents trained you out of bad table manners when you were growing up (I hope), you can train yourself out of poor goal manners right now. And all that "you can't teach an old dog new tricks" stuff? That was made up by people who were too lazy or scared to give themselves a worthy goal.

I think of the movie *Rocky II* when training myself for a tough goal. Rocky's trainer Mickey determines that in order to beat Apollo Creed, he actually needs to learn how to box right-handed, even though he's been a lefty his entire life. At first, it's really awkward and Rocky struggles re-learning how to box with a completely different hand. He wants to give up on it, but Mickey pushes him. Eventually, he does learn it and it throws Apollo Creed off completely. Your new goal will feel awkward to you at first because you are creating new brain pathways that are either dormant or never existed in the first place. Once they are locked in, however, it'll be just like knocking out Apollo Creed.

## Side Note: What's This Stuff about the Brain?

This brain stuff is worth mentioning. One of the reasons it's hard to learn new things is that your brain actually forms pathways like a worn groove in a carpet to the things you do all the time. Gymnasts have paths toward the parts of their brains that have to remember long and athletic routines. Singers have paths that lead toward controlling their vocal cords and their listening abilities. Writers have created paths between their hands and their words, allowing them to get quicker and more effective over time.

In the last decade or so, neuroscientists have determined that the brain can actually change its paths over time. If you are used to playing video games and you decide you want to use your free time to write instead, your brain can stop using the "video game path" as often and can start creating a "genius writer path" the more often you write. The best way to create this new path is to devote more time to your writing and make it a habit. It's hard at first, because it takes your brain a bit of time to dig out this new path, but once it's in there (about a month or so until the initial path is dug out) the sailing will be much smoother.

## Traits of a Strong Goal

People have the tendency to go at goals the wrong way. One of the big reasons for this is that there are many things in their lives they want to *stop* doing. As a result, their goals become somewhat negative like "I will not smoke" or "I will not watch television three hours a day." Goals don't work as well when they're negative because you still think about the area you're trying to avoid. In that television example you are still thinking about watching television and you are still thinking about the time of three hours a day. You want your brain to think about other things like writing. It's just like if I said, "don't think about a purple cow." You probably just pictured a purple cow in your mind. We need to take a different approach with our goals.

When you create a goal, leave out the words "not" or "don't" or similarly negative words. Keep it simple. For instance, "I will write for 30 minutes as soon as I get home from work every single day."

This goal can help you integrate writing into your life for a few reasons. The first is that it's positive. If you had been performing writing-blocking activities when you usually returned home like surfing the Internet or watching television, you would need to put those off to the side. Since you didn't even include those tasks in a negative way in your goal, you don't have to think about them.

The second strong aspect to this goal is that it's specific. By stating "30 minutes" and "every single day" you don't give yourself a lot of wiggle room. Time limits are important for goals because they are so much more attainable than something like "I will write a chapter every day" or "I will be nicer to people." You can look at a clock, put pen to paper and then stop when the clock hits 30 minutes. It is simple, specific and an easy habit for your brain to follow.

Thirdly, the goal requires that you do it every day. I am currently writing 2,000 words a day as part of my writing goal. Every day means Monday through Sunday, no excuses. When we force ourselves to do something only a few times a week it can be tough to make it a habit. If you want to wake up early every weekday, that's a fantastic goal. If you sleep in until noon on Saturday and Sunday, it's going to make it that much harder to wake up on Monday morning and continue your positive habit. When possible, and I realize that with fluctuating schedules, it's not always possible, try to integrate goals that you can do every day.

To recap, goals should be positive, specific and habitual.

## Side Note: Looking Weird

Some of the following methods to help a goal stick in your head have the possibility of making you look weird. Reading your goals out loud or sticking notes around the house for yourself might make your roommates or spouse insult you or give you strange looks. Setting big goals for yourself is the sort of thing that may ruffle the feathers of your friends and loved ones. Using some non-traditional methods to lock those goals into your brain may similarly rub people the wrong way. If you truly want something, don't let other people and their short-sighted thinking stop you. I have been mocked countless times for my goals and many people have told me they weren't worth it. I refused to believe them and now I am a playwright, a theatre producer, an actor and an author. Good thing I didn't let them get in my way.

## What Do I Do With It?

Say that you have picked your goal and you want to apply it to your life. There are many different ways to do this, which is fantastic because if one method doesn't work, you can totally ditch it and try another method. The main objective of any of these is to make the goal a habit. You're trying to create that pathway in your brain that will make the goal practically subconscious (i.e. doing it without thinking about it). Before a goal is a habit, you need to expend energy and will power to force yourself to do it. Once it is a habit, the goal becomes easier and you can spend your will power in other more productive ways.

One of the most effective ways to make your goal into a habit is to thoroughly memorize the goal and read it to yourself every day. Write your goal or goals out on a sheet of paper. Keep this paper by the side of your bed. Read the goal out loud to yourself each morning when you wake up and every night before you go to bed. This method allows the goal to circulate in your head all day and all night without you needing to expend much will power. Goal setting champion and author

Brian Tracy suggests re-writing out the goal each time before you read it to yourself. This is like reinforcing your goal with a thick layer of concrete. Writing the goals out gives your brain another thing to lock on to when creating this new habitual path.

To even further remind yourself of your goal, try writing the goal or goals out on a slip of paper and placing them in your wallet. My favorite place is right in front of my main debit card or even in front of my driver's license. This way, I am more likely to see the goal as often as possible whenever I open it up. Place notes around your house, cubicle or office that will continue to cement the goal in your mind. Since sticky notes can sometimes fall after a while, I suggest using index cards and tape.

While my side note above mentioned that some friends and family might hold you back from your goals, there are some who are more than willing to lend a hand. Find a goal buddy who is also looking to make an improvement in his life. Chat once a week about the goals that you've set and encourage each other to keep taking steps in the right direction. For example, if your goal is to find a publisher for your book proposal, your friend might advise you to make five phone calls a day to find out more information. He might drop you a quick text message saying, "Did you call them yet?" This personal method of encouragement can work much more effectively than a note if you find the right goal buddy.

Another method involving people is to create a Mastermind, which is like a support group of people who are there to help each other achieve their goals. Don't let the term "support group" throw you off, as it never hurts to have multiple people watching out for you and your best interests. Several best-selling authors like Marci Shimoff and Napoleon Hill thoroughly recommend these groups and write a few more words about them than I'll devote to the subject here.

Get creative with the ways you remind yourself of these important goals. Set your home page on the Internet to a Web page you create with your goal on it, change your computer Desktop to your goal, set up a text-message reminder service to send you your goal every day, tie a string around your finger, have your parents/children call you and remind you. There are many different ways to lock this goal into your head. Once it's in there, you are one step closer to being an author.

The best part about learning the *how* of setting goals is that all goals work the same way. If you lock the "I want to write my first book by January 1st" goal into your head you can likewise add the "I will promote my website 20 minutes each day" or the "I will train for a three mile race the next six months" or really any goals to your life. Like television and the Internet, you can become addicted to goal setting. A much healthier addiction if you ask me.

## Side Note: Covering All the Bases

We have a tendency to create blind spots in our lives. For instance, if you are used to heading out to the bars every weekday night with your work buddies, and you start setting these writing goals, you might automatically assume that the two hours you go out drinking are blocked out. You might not even think about it! If you skipped the bar a couple of nights a week, it might give you the time you need to start working on your book.

I have a friend who is the most goal-focused individual I've ever met personally. The guy is a former minor league baseball player, and a current trainer, professional speaker and a PhD in sociology. For years, he has had a notebook he uses to create and keep track of 25 major yearly goals and the minor goals that help him achieve the major ones. I had the fortune of flipping through the notebook a while back. There were some incredible goals about his speaking, coaching and income within the pages of that book. But there was something missing.

I had always heard my friend speak of his relationship with his significant other in hushed terms. While they had been dating a long time, it seemed that the two of them were no longer seeing eye-to-eye. As I looked at the yearly goals, many of them extremely admirable, I noticed that there were absolutely no goals about his love life.

When you are creating these writing and/or other goals for yourself, try to step back from your life or to get an outside opinion about the things you should be working on. This will help you to see the blind spots that you would normally overlook. You'll be a goal-achieving machine in no time.

## From a Goal to a Purpose

When I started setting goals in my own life, it was like a weight had been lifted off my small but capable shoulders. I no longer felt like I had to use will power alone to get things accomplished in my life. Setting tiny goals for my theatre producing and article writing made a world of difference for me. However, every couple of months, I would slip into similar patterns. The goals I had created started to slip away and I had no idea why. Usually, after another giant burst of will power I was able to set the goals up again, but I wondered why I had to expend so much energy after I'd created these wonderful habits for myself.

There are two reasons that these goals tended to slip through my fingers after a couple of months.

Imagine that you had been an Internet addict for the last three years. You are able to push this addiction off to the side after all that time and create some fantastic writing habits for yourself. Even after you've had this habit for three months, those paths in your brain that led to your love of the Internet are still there. For various reasons, you have to spend a lot of time on the Web one week and like that, you feel hooked again. Addiction occurs because the addicted person gets some sort of boost, usually hormonal like endorphins from doing the activity. When you accidentally get addicted to your negative habits again, you have to recognize the problem and start rebuilding the blocks for your goals again.

This is one of ways a support group or a goal buddy can help. They are the outsiders looking in on your life who can determine when you are falling back into old, negative habits. Having supportive people like this has helped me personally on many occasions.

The second reason is another pillar of support that can improve your goal setting, your overall attitude and your general direction. That pillar of support is having your goals protected by the umbrella of a life purpose.

What would life be like if you had a purpose as strong as Mother Theresa (helping people in need) or Thomas Edison (inventing products that improve the world)? Having a purpose is like having a super goal (a super objective as we call it in the acting biz) that pulls along all of your other goals. It is a fantastic litmus test for ensuring your smaller goals are correct. If you had the life purpose of "entertaining the world through your stories" than taking a new high-paying job in a legal office might not fit under that umbrella. If you are having trouble with a goal, seeing your purpose plastered on the wall, in your wallet or in your heart, can help you push past any procrastination to make it happen for the sake your higher function. Purpose leads to productivity.

How does one find this purpose? There is a simple exercise that I found on the first personal development site I ever visited, which is StevePavlina.com. Pavlina suggests that finding your purpose may not take years or an entire lifetime. It might actually take as little as 20 minutes.

Pull out a sheet of paper and a pencil or pen. I suggest a pencil because erasing may occur from time to time during this exercise. Write at the top of the sheet a heading along the lines of "My Purpose."

Write down a sentence or two about what you think your purpose might be. Just take a shot in the dark with the first thing that comes to mind. Read it out loud. Do you think that it completely fits? How does it make you feel? If it might not be 100% correct and you don't feel particularly inspired by it, try writing a revision of the previous statement.

Write. Revise. Write. Revise. Write. Revise, until …

You come upon a statement that makes tears well up in your eyes. Keep revising until you come up with a phrase that makes you say to yourself, "If I lived my life by that purpose, I would be happier, healthier and more driven." This can take a lot longer than 20 minutes and it may still not be perfect by the time you're through with it, but once you create something that tugs at your heartstrings a little, you are certainly going in the right direction.

Take this purposeful phrase that you have created and insert it into your memory and life using the same goal-memorization methods mentioned above. Write it on a sheet that goes in your wallet or by your bed. Spend some time reading it out loud to yourself. Heck, even write it into a notebook or a computer desktop that you use all of the time.

Having a purpose locked into your brain can really make the goals like writing your first book, flow a lot more smoothly. Though I used to be more of a go with the flow kind of person, I'd much rather be a "go with the creative flow that comes from having a strong purpose" kind of guy.

## Side Note: Sprinkle It with Sugar

Creating goals or a purpose is helped by two major personality aspects that are inseparably intertwined. Those two traits are faith and optimism.

By faith, I'm not referring to religious or spiritual faith per say. But I am saying that if you don't put some amount of trust into the possibility of your goals and purpose working for you, you're going to be sunk. If you are trained to be a pessimist who says, "I'll try this but it probably won't work for me," then it's going to be hard for you to trust anything including yourself.

When I started personal development I left myself completely open to new belief systems, because it was obvious that my current one was not working. This allowed me to try out things like training my subconscious with goals and the Law of Attraction and other things that a stubborn person might choose not to believe in. When it comes down to it, I had a faith that things could be better for me than they already were. Just having that faith pushed me in the right direction.

Optimism is tough for some people. True optimism is trusting that things can be better whether your current circumstances are good or bad. This is a major aspect of what Marci Shimoff refers to as "Happy for No Reason" in her book of the same name. I cannot recommend her book highly enough as it helped me to understand what happiness really was.

Happiness is not about your circumstances. If that were the case, all the rich people who were movie superstars or won the lottery would be happy and all the people who endured horrible accidents and poor life conditions would be miserable. Since that's not the case, we have to change our assumptions about happiness. According to Marci, happiness comes in part from within and in part from training. Yes, you can actually train yourself to be happy instead of being a grump.

Looking around for the gift in every tough situation, eating healthier foods and exercising, laughing and smiling with positively-minded friends, and believing that you have a little bit of help from upstairs are just a few of the ways that you can become an optimistic person.

Adding a pinch of faith and a dash of optimism to your goals and purpose will improve your chances of becoming an author tremendously.


## How to Keep Inspired

Let's say that you're keeping a checklist of all the things I've been talking about. You have created some goals for yourself. Check. You have created some supporting goals in other categories that might improve your energy like eating more healthily. Check. You have done the purpose exercise and you have hand-crafted an overarching umbrella to protect your goals. Check. You have even read books like *Happy for No Reason* by Marci and *Learned Optimism* by Martin Seligman to improve your levels of faith and optimism. Check.

On many days, this recipe for success is going to work without a hitch. But just like cooking, sometimes you need to add a little bit of salt or spice to make it right.

That salt and spice is motivation or inspiration.

I didn't really understand the concept of motivation until I started listening to personal development audio tapes (or CDs or MP3s, etc.). I would be chugging along just fine on my writing when all of a sudden my old cravings for the Internet or sugary foods or something, anything other than writing would knock me off track. As per the suggestion of Pavlina and other authors, I started listening to audio programs as a bit of inspiration in the middle of the day.

The change was instantaneous. I listened to programs like Earl Nightingale's "Lead the Field" and Tom Butler-Bowdon's "50 Success Classics" when I either felt burned out or had a little bit of downtime. These programs and programs similar to them are completely full of wisdom. The downtrodden feeling I had experienced before turning these programs on was completely lifted away within just a few minutes. Hearing about these concepts of success made me feel like I could be successful and those old, antsy feelings just floated away.

While before these audio programs, I could only work for about an hour at a time before I felt too anxious and overwhelmed to continue, these programs helped me to work for several hours (with a few audio intermissions) without stopping.

If you aren't into audio programs or you have had no luck milking them for inspiration, there are plenty of other methods to pump you up when you're feeling a little low. I have heard stories of people who post inspirational quotes from their favorite authors, humorists and famous people that make them feel strong and confident. It's easy to find such quotes, as a simple online search will yield thousands of them. Take your pick of quotes and either print them out on a sheet of paper or write them on a sticky note or index card. Place them all around your house, in your wallet and on your computer to get occasional bursts of inspiration throughout the day. Change out the quotes every so often to keep them fresh.

While online video sites like YouTube can be major time drainers, they are also the source of many
inspirational videos. I love pulling up speeches from TED (Technology Entertainment and Design) which has featured speakers like Tony Robbins, Al Gore, Elizabeth Gilbert and plenty of brilliant people you've never heard of. These speeches get your mind working again after the gears have grinded to a halt. There are also plenty of videos from motivators like Zig Ziglar, Jim Rohn and Oprah Winfrey that can likewise make you feel like a million bucks.

Back in the early days of self-help, the tale of the tape was to list the achievements of people who achieved major success in their lives. These people could be famous or they could simply be those who came from poverty or hardship to achieve greatness. I can honestly say that hearing the powerful and motivated tales of these people also has the ability to inspire and motivate throughout the day. A simple Web search for "success stories" or "inspirational stories" or "successful people" will yield you with enough material to stay motivated for the rest of the year. Some paper sources of these stories include books by Orison Swett Marden and Samuel Smiles.

There is no way for me to burrow directly into your head and find out what inspires you, so it is up to you to figure out if audio programs, quotes, videos, stories or something completely different are right for you. These bits of inspiration throughout your week, month and year can improve your productivity dramatically. Before you know it, you could blow through your first book and be on to your second in much less time that you thought possible.

## Using Your Day

Now that you have some methods for getting your motor revving, it's time to learn all of the tips and tricks possible to use during your busy 9 to 5 lifestyle. I have broken down the next few chapters into the morning, afternoon, evening and weekend, but all of these times can be extremely adapted if your eight or more hours of work are at a different time. I don't want you graveyard shift people to feel like I'm leaving you out!

As I mentioned before, there are many different tricks you can use in your quest to be an author and I'm going to list any and all I can think of. You don't need to use all of them at once. Heck, I don't think I've ever used all of them at once. Simply adopt a few and your productivity will improve dramatically. All of the ideas I put forth will be most effective when supported by the foundation of goals and purpose. If you have yet to lock those in, I would stop reading until you get to that point. I want you to have the best chance possible to succeed and if it takes re-reading this chapter several times, so be it.

You've been warned. Now, let's move on to the morning.

# 3 THE MORNING

When I was growing up, I was always impressed by my father and how well he used his time in the morning to prepare himself for the day. By the time my family and I would get up, he would have worked out, gotten his papers together for teaching his seventh grade earth science students and had his stylish work clothes pressed and ready. I am fortunate enough to have gotten some genes in this area from his side (my mom and brother are both late night owls conversely). I know that not everybody is a morning person and I realize that to some, just getting up in the morning can feel like the hardest part of the day.

Fortunately for all of us, the brain is malleable. You can change almost anything about yourself with a little bit of training. I am, in part, going to tell you some methods that will trim the fat. This includes cutting out the number of snooze alarms that you hit in order to feel awake quicker so that you can improve your early morning productivity. Enough chitter chatter: let's get started.

## Early Morning: 6 AM to 8 AM

The sun is about to rise and the world is hard at work. Newspapers are being delivered in bundles, produce is being washed and sorted, and you are rolling out of bed. Why are you getting up so damn early? The morning is a perfect time to get some work finished. There are fewer distractions, you probably don't have anywhere to be, and your brain is rested and ready to turn on. Most people getting up this early would fall asleep in their oatmeal, and you might start that way too. You will learn to make it work for you, however, and here are some ideas that will help you to use the morning to your advantage.


## Waking Up

Most of us are trained to hit the snooze button several times before we look up at the clock, say "aw &*%#," throw on our clothes haphazardly and then head to work a semi-disheveled mess. You have chosen this pattern for yourself and you can change it. It will be hard at first but you can make it work.

Start by setting more than one alarm. Use a second clock, a third clock, your cell phone, your computer, a wake-up call service, etc. Put the alarms far enough away from your bed that you have to get up. Make sure they are annoying enough to shock you into life. The first few times you employ this method it will be quite jolting, but the body and mind are quite resilient and they will adjust to the routine. The more often you do it, you will create a new path in your brain for waking up more effectively.

Make additions to the plan as necessary. If you live with your partner, employ him or her to motivate you. Tell him or her that you are trying to be more productive. Chances are your partner will be on your side and can give you the occasional last shove to get out of bed. Leave yourself a positive note by your second alarm reminding you of what you're trying to do. If you are unable to get up one morning, just keep trying new things until it works, and at some point it will.

Another method you can incorporate in this effort (and in all of your goals throughout the day) is positive visualization. Set aside a bit of time each day before you go to bed to imagine your morning. See the alarm going off and you finding yourself wide awake to turn it off and get out of bed. As you visualize yourself rising up with no trace of tiredness whatsoever, feel a sense of accomplishment and joy at having succeeded at waking. Visualization can be a little silly, but it's totally in keeping with having a bit of faith and trust as I mentioned in Chapter 2. Trust that some of these wacky methods can work and you'll find yourself pushing far ahead of the haters who don't believe in anything at all.

How early you get up is totally up to you. I like leaving myself one to two hours of productivity before work. Once up, use your normal bathroom routine and know, just know, that what you're doing is good. And now, if you don't hate me too much for disturbing your beauty sleep let's start activating that brain of yours.

## Natural Energy

The first instinct for many people is to head straight to the coffee pot, which is set to brew an inordinately large amount of brew at this time of the day. I don't recommend it. In fact, I recommend a morning without coffee, Red Bull, soda or anything else laced with chemicals that alter the brain. I know that there are many studies about the benefits of caffeine and there are just as many about it causing you harm.

Let's face it, most of those studies show people that are drinking caffeine at normal levels. With all of the added espresso shots, multiple cups and various sources of caffeine we tend to indulge in, we are falling beyond the scope of those studies. Caffeine works by blocking your adrenaline receptors so that adrenaline can bounce around your system keeping you alert. I personally picture this adrenaline as little wrecking balls bouncing around with no place to go. I think of the crash that comes after the wrecking balls have beat up my system and are finally at rest. Maybe it's just me, but after the caffeine crash, I feel bad and I don't like feeling bad.

When I quit coffee and caffeine in general, I had a tough few months of staying awake in the morning. But eventually, my natural mechanisms kicked back into place and I felt clearer than I ever did during my caffeine phase. I felt natural and healthy and most importantly, I felt more creative. In order to tap into your natural creativity, you've got to keep it real. Here are some non-caffeinated morning options for you:

A breakfast of fruit, nuts, and juice, a workout of cardiovascular endurance, strength training or both, a guided or self-meditation, rocking out to your favorite energized music, a small trip to your nearest body of water or other inspiring location.

## Natural Energy Option #1: Healthy Breakfast

First, let's talk about the healthy breakfast. We are a little bit silly sometimes us humans. We tend to go for the quickest and tastiest breakfast possible but we don't always think about how it will affect our energy later. While waffles and pastries and donuts are really, really good, they will kick our butts a few hours (or less) after we eat them. One of the best natural sources of energy to thwart this problem is fruit. This raw and tasty food is like nature's pastry. A plate full of berries, apples, bananas and melons in the morning includes vitamins, fiber and micronutrients that all contribute positively to your day. Supplement that with some nuts, which are high in the protein and the good fats (monounsaturated fats) which are fantastic for energy and for the brain. Add a little bit of juice, the kind that's not from concentrate and full of added sugar and you've got yourself an energy packed little breakfast.

## Natural Energy Option #2: Workout

I was a wrestler in high school and among the crazy things we did like wearing headgear and singlets and beating each other up on the mat, we would work out before school at 5:30 a.m. My first class of the day was American History and after exercising I always felt like I was buzzing the entire 45 minutes. Everything made sense and my brain seemed to be moving at light speed. It was the first class that I truly aced in school and it inspired me to work hard and get into a decent school for undergrad.

Years later, when I found out that working out increases the flow of oxygen to your brain, it made complete sense. All the facts and figures clicked so easily during that class and it was in part a result of my morning exercise. Exercise also increases the amount of endorphins in your body, which are like nature's happiness hormones. We've already discussed how much happiness and optimism can improve your goal setting. Imagine combining a faster, smarter brain with a healthy dose of optimism. That's what it's like to get a morning workout in.

You can join a gym, go for a run, or do an at home program like P90X (which is extremely hardcore but it really is a kick in the pants for your physical health). Even just a 20 minute workout with some push-ups, sit-ups and a few jumping jacks can make a world of difference for you energy-wise. Because working out has been so beneficial to my writing, I see my exercise goals as a perfect complement to my writing goals. Exercise improves my energy throughout the day and makes me a smarter and more efficient writer by far.

## Natural Energy Option #3: Meditation

"Uh-oh, Bryan, we're getting into the weird stuff," you might be thinking. It's true, a lot of people think meditation and meditative exercise like yoga, tai-chi or qigong are weird. But it's also true that those people don't get to experience the many benefits of meditation.

I think that the most important aspect of meditation is that it can improve your focus. In our over-caffeinated, over-stimulated world, additional focus can go a long way. Typically, the bad decisions we make like eating that extra donut or surfing around on the Web too much can be thwarted by stepping back and focusing on what we really want. You always hear stories about someone coming upon an amazing idea during a moment of clarity. Meditation is like a training manual that can turn those moments into minutes and those minutes into days worth of clarity.

Imagine if you could come up with brilliant ideas throughout your day. That is what a life is like on meditation. Meditation also has been shown to improve your levels of happiness through stimulating the hormones that promote happiness in your body. A little meditation in your morning can go a long way.

There are classes available in meditation along with guided audio meditations and many resources online. Finding the right meditation for you is like finding the right pair of shoes. One might fit but not feel so good when you walk around with it for a while. Experiment until you find a meditation routine for you and try to work it into your morning.

## Natural Energy Option #4: Rocking Out

This is a simple method for an energy boost in the morning. Make a little playlist of your favorite upbeat songs and get your groove on. The greatest advantage to this method is that within three minutes (the length of the average pop song) you can get yourself out of a morning funk and ready to face your morning writing tasks and your day of work. Keep in mind that some genres (80s synthesizer music) tend to work better than others (sad country music).

To add to the potential silliness of this method, try dancing about and really getting into the music. If you live with people, this might not be as possible, but you can always shut the door to your room and have a few minutes of *Dancing with the Stars* to yourself.

One thing to keep in mind with music is that you may become used to a particular song to the point that it doesn't pump you up anymore. Luckily for you, there are plenty of songs in the sea and you can always find another that will leave you feeling wonderful.

## Natural Energy Option #5: Location and Inspiration

Another way in which I'm fortunate is that I live just a 15 minute walk away from Lake Michigan, which can be quite a beautiful site during the warmer months. It obviously depends on where you live, but if you can find yourself an awe-inspiring place within walking distance of your house, you may be able to grab a bit of morning peace from it.

Even before the work day officially begins, it's easy to get caught up in e-mail, projects and meetings that you might have a hard time stepping back and thinking about anything creative. It's finding this "spot of Zen" that allows you to relax and not think about anything at all for a minute or two that can get you fresh and energized.

Even if you are in an awful, dingy location, there is always a sunrise and if you get up that early every once in a while, you can gain some peace from taking 10 minutes to soak it all in.


You can use one of these ideas, mix and match, or throw your own into the hat. Personally, I've done them all but I've most often done the raw meal of fruits, nuts and juice and the workout. All of these methods can wake your brain up sans chemicals. You may not feel as high as when you are on the caffeine, but you will still be awake enough to be productive.

What if you do one of these methods and you're still having trouble waking up? Then you should keep trying the other methods until you wake up. If you spend the whole early morning period completing these natural energy tasks and then you have to go to work without getting anything productive done, this is still a perfectly good use of your time.

In *Seven Habits of Highly Effective People*, Stephen Covey talks about the value of doing Quadrant II activities. These are tasks that are important but not urgent that will help your production capability, which is essentially the efficiency of how you get your work done. If you spent every morning building your energy in such a natural way using so many different methods that would be one hell of a routine. Soon enough you'd be in better shape, more positive, and more inspired. Sounds like a great situation to be in.

Incorporate more natural energy into your life/morning and less chemical energy and your brain will thank you for it.

## Side Note: A Quiet Place

One of the most difficult aspects of working from home, even if it's just for half an hour in the morning is that there are too many distractions. I do not yet have a family of my own, as it is just myself and my girlfriend, but I still feel pulled in a few different directions in the morning. The ideal situation for your morning thinking, writing and other activities is to find a quiet place.

If you have the ability to set aside an office space with a door that can close or lock, this is the most effective space to work in. Not everybody has that many rooms or an office space that can be closed off from the rest of the house or apartment. Setting up a small desk somewhere in the house is another option. Try to put your foot down about not being disturbed during a particular time to avoid distractions while writing.

An option that I have found helpful is to visit a local coffee shop or grocery store with free Wi-Fi (or at the least, free electrical outlets) with my laptop or a pencil and paper. These locations are often open very early and if there are any close by or on your way to work, they might function as a nice third location that you do most of your writing work in.

Try your best to avoid distractions wherever you write or think in order to be as efficient as possible. Also, make sure your significant other, children or roommates understand how important writing is to you and why it's tough for you to deal with distractions. That's a much better option than getting pissed off at them when they distract you without them really knowing why.

## Think

There's no better way to utilize your now awake mind then to sit down and think. You may use this thinking time in several ways. You can plan out the rest of your morning and your day. You can brainstorm about the writing project you are working on. You can start thinking about a particular part of your life that needs work, like your finances or your relationships. Or you can just take out a sheet of paper and write whatever comes to you. A huge reason that thinking should be a part of your morning is that it will stimulate your brain to think all the day long.

Work and life can be filled with so many tasks that you can accomplish on autopilot. Taking the train, sending an e-mail and filling out a tedious form are just a few of many. By actually thinking early on in your day, you give yourself the option of actively using your brain instead of letting it use you.

You can also save time on the task you are about to accomplish if you have a better idea of how to attack it. Another Steven Covey-ism is that it doesn't matter how much progress you are making chopping through the brush in the jungle if you aren't even in the right jungle to begin with. Thinking beforehand can help you make sure that what you plan on doing is worth your time.

It is very important that you write these thoughts down instead of just thinking them in your head. You are much more likely to remember your thoughts, especially the important ones if you write them down and keep them in a notebook or somewhere else that is protected. The major ideas for this book came from some notes I wrote down over six months ago. It would have been tough for me to remember all the intricate details if I hadn't written them down somewhere special. In addition, by using your hands instead of just your brain, you are actually stimulating your brain more, which may help you to think more creatively.

It can be difficult for someone who hasn't taken notes in a while to get into a thinking state. If you can't think of anything to write, simply write facts about yourself or things that need to get done. You could write, "I am an accountant, but I want to be a writer." Even just a fact like this could help you get in the swing of thinking. It might lead to a thought like "It would be fun to write a book about a part-detective, part-accountant" or "I don't have much work today, why don't I leave an hour early to write." Writing anything at all may be enough to get you hooked on thinking (a very healthy addiction).

## Act

You have thought about what to do and now you have to make it happen. You know the best method for you. Whether it is creating an outline, brainstorming a character, or just plain diving into the thing, push forward and don't look back. By this time, the sun may be poking up and the time is getting closer and closer to when you need to leave for work. Do not let this distract you. You have time and you should use it.

If you only have a limited amount of time at this point, say ten minutes or so, just get something down on paper. Do not over think; the thinking has been done already. Get yourself into the habit of at least getting something done. This way, little by little, you can accomplish your goal.

If you have the day off or you don't work until later in the day, this "Act" stage can go on indefinitely. Keep energized with natural forms of energy and take short breaks if you need to. I will discuss longer periods of free time in the later chapter about writing on the weekend.

When you have sufficiently acted or it is time to get going, start getting ready for work. You may feel accomplished and you may not, but if you keep working towards your goal, you will eventually look for bigger and scarier challenges to get up early for.

## Mid-Morning: 8 AM to 10 AM

You've made it through the bright and early first part of the morning. You either accomplished part of a goal or you have begun to pave the way to your own style of daily motivation. Some people will be able to stay at home and continue to cultivate their productivity. Most of the world, however, will be suiting up, buttoning up, or packing up on their way to their nine to five jobs. Being a creative person shackled with a non-creative job can be a tough situation for getting things done. Since your boss might frown upon you moonlighting as an author while you're supposed to be filing forms, there are some small steps you can take to use your time wisely without getting any nasty looks or pink slips.

Many nine to five workers spend this time period sipping their coffee and trying to get focused on their days. Since you have already accomplished this in the early morning, you can utilize these couple of hours to increase your daily motivation and as a result, your productivity will probably rub off on your eight hour a day job as well. The name of the game in this section is learning, planning, and idea generation.

## Going to Work

If you live in the big city like I do, you probably take the train or the bus to work. If you go out to the suburbs or you do not have such a transportation system, you might take a car. These methods of transportation are a perfect opportunity for learning.

More often than not, I see people zoning out on their iPods or listening to loud music or a somewhat funny morning program on their car radios. There is an opportunity being missed here. There are some great audio programs out there that deal specifically with all subsets of personal development. There are programs on motivation, success, spiritual well-being, etc. Instead of using this audio listening time to space out, it can be used to strengthen our minds.

These types of programs are available all over the Internet, can be downloaded or checked out from your public library, or purchased at bookstores. Not all of them will resonate with you, but if you find one that you truly believe can help you improve yourself, it can leave you with a great feeling by the time you reach work. Also, a positive side-effect of a high-quality program is that you will feel more motivated for the next several hours. I suggest looking for a program on success, personal development, creativity, or any area you've wanted to develop.

## Side Note: My Favorite Programs

As I mentioned earlier, there are some audio programs that I have found enormously helpful to keep me motivated and inspired throughout the day. One of the first programs I ever listened to was Earl Nightingale's "Lead the Field." Nightingale was one of the pioneers of personal development audio in the 1950s and 1960s and as a result, some of his work is a bit dated. Nevertheless, the man does a fantastic job of condensing many ideas of personal development into an easy to understand package. He also has a deep, resonating voice that makes you feel as though you're being spoken to by a wise, old sage.

For the person without the time to read some of the great classics of motivation, Tom Butler-Bowdon's work is especially intriguing. In his books *50 Success Classics*, *50 Self-Help Classics* and *50 Prosperity Classics*, Butler-Bowdon offers a 10 minute version of these classics with a modern viewpoint. Listening to an entire work condensed into its most important points is like taking a shot of mental wheatgrass: healthy, concentrated and powerful. I've learned about old and new works I never would have heard of otherwise. This is the perfect audio companion if you only have a few minutes to spare, as each bit of the book is jam-packed with wisdom and knowledge.

Marci Shimoff, the only of my personal development gurus I've had the pleasure of speaking with, is like the queen of happiness. Her book, *Happy for No Reason* has made me a healthier and more joyful person by far. Whenever I feel myself slipping into the muck of depression, I pop her book into my MP3 player and I spend the entire week listening to and acting on her ideas and anecdotes of the "Happy 100" as she calls them (100 truly happy people from the inside-out). I do have to recommend that you buy the Recorded Books version of the book, as it is the unabridged version and has more stories and exercises than the regular audio version.

Other wonderful audio books include Tony Robbins' *Awaken the Giant Within*, *The Celestine Prophecy* by James Redfield (which is like an adventure personal development book) and *The Secret* by Rhonda Byrne.

## The Daily Plan

You have arrived at work. It's time to get situated and sit down at the desk to start plugging away. Right? Not quite yet.

This is a good opportunity for you to plan out your day, both for your time at work and afterward. While you could spend a few minutes talking to your co-workers or get your eyes adjusted to the dim lights of the computer screen, getting a solid itinerary is going to be the most helpful for your motivation. Making this plan is the best way to find gaps in the work day where you could do some writing, a lunch break perhaps, or to figure out things that need to be accomplished after work that could get in your way of your writing time. If you can plan to knock all the required tasks out of the way, quickly and efficiently, you allow yourself to be more excited about getting the chance to write, instead of thinking that you'll never get around to it. It is much more comforting if you can see the way that it'll happen.

I doubt that your boss will stop you from doing this planning session, even though it happens to extend to the entire day. Tell him it helps you think and it makes you a more efficient and productive employee. If he forbids you this several minute activity, get to work a few minutes early, sit down in the lobby or at a café around the corner and plan before you go inside.

One of my favorite planning methods came from my goal-oriented friend I mentioned earlier. He would write out all of his goals from the day and then place a one, a two or a three next to each one. The items with a one next to them were goals that were the most important to him by far. They wouldn't necessarily be the most urgent, but they were the most important to get done to achieve his larger goals. The goals with a two were still important but slightly less so and the three's were like bonus goals that could be taken care of if time permitted.

If your work life is too complicated to fit in your outside-of-work planning, I suggest that you get a second notebook just for your writing. This will help you to keep work and your creative masterpiece separate. This will also help you to keep from feeling overwhelmed every time you open your planner. Just pencil in what writing and brainstorming time you can. Remember, a little bit every day goes a long way toward achieving your goal.


## The Note Pad

This is a simple but often overlooked step for a desk employee. Have a note pad available to jot down any ideas that you might generate during the day. Sometimes the doldrums of the office can make you forget some of your stronger ideas and it's important to not let them go. One idea can lead to another and before you know it, forgetting one good thought can make you miss out on an entire screenplay or novel.

One of the more time-consuming requirements to achieve a degree in Dramatic Arts from my school was the course labeled Production Practicum. In this class, which was really more of an unpaid internship, we had to work on the technical side of the University's professional company for about five weeks. This essentially kept us out of acting or directing in any of the student shows. Overachievers like me, decided to do Production Practicum over Spring Break so that we'd miss fewer student theatre opportunities.

During the long days of tech week, I was stationed up in the light booth for multiple 10 hour days while the stage manager and director worked on setting the cues for a production of *Uncle Vanya*. Almost out of boredom, I had a few sheets of paper on which to jot down notes for school or otherwise. As I began to watch the play for around the tenth time, I started to come up with ideas for a full-length play myself. I began to draw parallels between *Vanya* and my own life, setting the play in a dorm room instead of the country.

My notes later became a script, which I had the fortune of producing twice, once in college and once in 2010. If I had not given myself the option to jot down notes which consisted of plot points and bits of dialogue, I might not have ever put together this play.

In the play, *Glen Garry Glen Ross*, the salesmen at the firm have the phrase "always be closing" as a motto. In the writing world it's more like "always be creating." The more you create over time, whether it be through notes jotted down into a little book or actual stories, it can lead to something huge. Give yourself the option to create while you are at work. Even one idea a week is 52 ideas more than a person without a notebook might have.

It's helpful to develop a little shorthand system for yourself so you're not spending more time writing notes than working. At the end of the day you can review your notes and see if you thought of anything life-changing. If not, any idea has the chance to be used later.

If you tend to have a lot of ideas, they can really add up. An idea an hour leads to forty ideas per week, 160 per month, and 1,920 a year. At least one of them is bound to be good.

## Late Morning: 10 AM to 12 PM

This is the time when most employees during which the coffee has kicked in, the salutations and donut offerings have ceased, and the real work is getting done. I do not expect a lot of writing or idea generation to be accomplished during this time, but there are still a couple items that can be addressed to further improve your daily motivation for writing as a whole.

## The Workspace

What do you have at your desk and cubicle area? Pictures of family? A funny office joke from a couple of months ago? A plant? The real question isn't what you have there but how it makes you feel. Does that old Far Side comic taped to your monitor make you feel happy or cynical? Does that picture of a beautiful beach inspire you to go there for vacation or are you using it as one of those "this probably won't happen but at least a man can dream" sort of pictures?

My suggestions for your work space: a vision board and your goals. A vision board is used along with the Law of Attraction to help you visualize things that you want to happen to you in the world. If you want to be wealthy, you put up pictures of the objects you would have if you were wealthy like an extravagant house, a yacht, and a huge television. At this point, when you look at the board, you must visualize yourself as if you already have these items and the positive feeling that results from that situation. The belief of the law of attraction is that by doing this exercise you will attract those things toward you. If you *wish* that you had the items or you get angry at yourself for not having them, the board will have the opposite effect and you will push those items farther away.

Putting up your goals can be a great tool to remind yourself why you want to stay motivated. If your goal is to make enough money at your job so that you own a bigger family house, you could type up the phrase, "I want to create a better life for my family," and post it on your cubicle wall. If you want to write a novel, post up, "I will write a novel by the end of 2012." Once again, just like the vision board, do not get angry if this hasn't happened already, you must think positively. By surrounding yourself with your goals, it's like having a sip of motivation every time you look up. As if you thought, "what am I still going on for?" and you looked up to find the answers all around you.

## Side Note: The Law of Attraction

Alright, I've mentioned the Law of Attraction several times without really getting into it. This is one of those sorts of spiritual theories that some people are automatically turned off by when they read personal development books for the first time. As I mentioned before, this was one of those theories I decided to adopt because it was a more effective world view than the one I already had. Imagining that even when things were rough, they could be explained and they could be overcome with joy and the right kind of visualization is a heck of a lot better than hopelessness.

When you boil it down to its essence, the Law of Attraction is about being grateful for what you have and grateful for what you want to have in the future. This means that even if you have hardships in your life, you make your best effort to be grateful and joyful about it. At the same time, you also visualize the things you want, like the career of a bestselling author, a hearty paycheck and a happy life with your family and friends. While visualizing those wonderful things, you also attempt to express joy and gratitude, as if these positive events have already arrived.

In theory, you project this joy and these wants out into the Universe and at some point these things you desire will come to you if you keep a positive and optimistic attitude.

Talking about this subject reminds me of the Nicholas Cage movie "National Treasure" when Cage's character and his partner Riley (played hilariously by Justin Bartha) are attempting to convince a government employee that someone is trying to steal the Declaration of Independence. Riley's line "And that's where we lost the Homeland Security," is how I feel when I'm describing the Law of Attraction.

Yes, the Law of Attraction seems like one part prayer, one part magic and one part craziness. However, there are so many people who have had a positive impact from it (including yours truly) that it is important to include in a book that involves getting motivated and what you want. There are many people out there who might not need something metaphysical like the Law of Attraction. They might be able to set their goals, achieve them and have a book in seemingly no time at all.

The Law of Attraction is for the people who don't know the "how." They have no idea "how" they are going to finish their book. They have no idea "how" they can possibly create the time to fit in writing even a single chapter. The Law of Attraction is all about not knowing how something will occur but picturing it with gratitude anyway.

Many of the kinds of things you'd put on a vision board are the things you have no idea how to get. A beautiful new house, a life on the beach and a best-selling novel get placed on this board because you want them in your life and you are leaving it up to the Universe to nudge your life in that direction. If you spend a little bit of time each day to think about what you want in your life in a joyful and excited way, the theory is that the Universe will recognize this and will find a way to make it happen for you.

You don't even have to believe in it to try it. I simply suggest that you try it for a month and see if anything interesting happens. And now back to the show.


## The Smart Snack

You may not be hungry at this point in the day quite yet, but it is a good idea to eat a little bit now to avoid eating a huge lunch. By eating a healthy snack, such as a banana, some nuts, and a little bit of unbuttered popcorn, you can really take the edge off of lunch and you can keep your brain fueled for the rest of the morning. When I work at an office I like to keep little snacks with me all day long to keep myself at peak energy and motivation.

This snack can help you feel positive and full. If you eat a smaller lunch as a result of the snack you will help yourself around the problem of the post-lunch slump. For the snack I suggest keeping it below 300 calories and sticking to foods with few to no preservatives.

Some options include: a bag of trail mix, an all-natural protein bar, a yogurt parfait, an apple and a banana, raw almonds, and whole wheat crackers and cheese.


## Taking a Moment

Staring at a screen all day can take a lot out of you. I've had nine hour days of data entry before that have caused me to want to flop on a couch and get as much rest as possible before the next day of the same task. While some people have trouble getting into writing on the side as a result of poor planning and a lack of drive, others are just plain beat up by the time they get home. One of the best ways to preserve your energy is to take little breaks of less than a minute to keep your system working effectively.

Either look outside of the window or close your eyes. Clear your mind of any task that you're working on. Breathe in through your nose for at least three seconds. Put a smile on your face and then exhale.

Inhale and exhale in the same manner at least three times. If any thoughts of work or pessimism creep in just imagine that you're breathing them out with the exhalation. Repeat this exercise as many times as you need and then dive back into your work.

Taking a moment for yourself in the middle of a hectic morning, even though it seems like a tiny blip on the radar, can save you a great deal of energy for later. The smiling portion is a tiny burst of endorphins that can help you to release some of the tension that has built up already during your day. Imagine yourself as an engine that from time to time begins to overheat. Letting a little steam out every so often can improve your engine life and prevent it from breaking down.

In addition to the relaxing effect, this may also act as a perfect time to work in a little bit of positive visualization or at the least to say one of your key goals out loud or internally to yourself. Picturing the positive outcome of all your work or the writing on the side goal you have to look forward to when you return home can increase your work productivity and make you feel more upbeat.

## Conclusion

The clock has struck noon and you are feeling pretty good about yourself. After working through some bumps in the road, you have actually stayed motivated and happy from 6 AM to 12 PM. This is the hardest part of the day for most people and if you are able to achieve this state in the morning more often than not, you are well on your way to being a motivated writer on the side. A strong, productive morning lays a great foundation for the afternoon and especially the evening.

I sometimes like to look at the process of daily motivation like keeping a balloon from hitting the ground. A good naturally energized breakfast pushes the balloon into the air, some thinking and productive work hits it up as gravity pulls it downward and the words of someone like Earl Nightingale smacks it once again above the floor of negativity and laziness. It can be annoying to continually hit the balloon and at times it can get discouraging, but if you are diligent in your balloon whacking, you will get more done every single day.

Try some of these ideas and techniques for 30 days and see if they help you. The worst that can happen is that you still feel crappy and detached at work. The best is that you can actually fit writing back into your work days.

# 4 THE AFTERNOON

After a good amount of practice with the morning's daily motivation, you have finally reached noon with a full head of steam. While the first part of the day is often the hardest, keeping yourself going through the lull of the afternoon can be a challenge. Most people will eat a big lunch, perhaps with another hit of caffeine and be ready for a nap by around 2:30 to 3 PM. If you are going to get through work and be prepared to write a little in the evening, you must take a different route. A lot of your afternoon work involves maintaining your positive energy from the morning, taking strides towards evening productivity, and just plain being healthy.

## Early Afternoon: 12 PM to 2 PM

### Lunch of Champions

The typical office lunch is a starved grabbing of a heavy sandwich mixed with the leftovers you brought from the previous night. Often there is little to no eating after breakfast, so you stuff yourself silly with as much food as you can put down. This food then sets off a program in your brain to divert more energy to digestion and less to thought.

The mind wanders as the stomach churns and the afternoon is all but lost.

But you will do better.

If you'll remember, during the first half of the day, you had a smart snack to keep your energy up and to prevent the need for a huge lunch. If you have taken this intelligent step, why ruin it with a mammoth meal? Gather yourself a nice and healthy plate, with as many fruits and vegetables as you can scrape together. Keep the meal under 500 calories if you can, but a ton of healthy calories can trump that rule if you're starving. Stay away from the sugary snacks and the high preservatives (frozen microwaveable meals are full of them) and you will notice something strange at the end of your break.

You aren't tired. You actually feel rejuvenated instead of stuffed and sleepy. Remember that feeling, because you won't always be perfect with this step if you have to order in from a fast food joint every so often. If you can remind yourself of how it feels when you eat a Lunch of Champions, you'll work hard to make it happen again.


## A Few Minutes Alone

While occasionally you may be required to go off to lunch with a client or as part of a departmental bonding session, more often than not you have the choice of what you want to do during your lunch. If you have an hour to eat and you only take 20 minutes to finish your food, you can spend those 40 minutes however you want.

If you go out to lunch with friends and colleagues, that segment of time will be given over to talking about the office, television that was on the previous night and various other items of chit chat. I am not suggesting that you dispense with that time completely, but I am saying that even if you just take a few minutes for yourself, you can get some writing done or you can do a few energy boosting activities.

Save time during lunch by either packing it or buying something on your way in and putting it in the fridge. The less time you spend during your break, the more you'll have to try on one of these afternoon activities.

## Afternoon Activity #1: Write 200 Words

As I mentioned earlier, I have been writing 2,000 words per day, which takes me anywhere between an hour and two and a half hours. While it is ideal to make major progress on your book every day, even as much as one-tenth of 2,000 can move you closer to your goal.

200 words usually consists of a paragraph or two and it might take anywhere between 10 and 45 minutes, though that can vary considerably depending on what you're writing. Don't worry so much about it being disjointed from anything you've previously written, since the hardest part about a book is just finishing the first draft. Get it finished through these bite-size 200 word chunks over the course of many lunches and you can fix it up later.

For this activity, I suggest a corner of the lunch room without any people, a nearby café, or even your own desk if people won't bother you with work-related inquiries while you're there.

To track your progress, use the word count tool on your word processor program if using a computer, or make an estimate using how many words are typically in a line and counting the number of lines on a sheet of paper.

I understand that things come up at lunch sometimes and you may not be able to make the habit an everyday thing. Just keep in mind that every 200 words you write bring you closer to a finished product.

## Afternoon Activity #2: Character Description

Let's say that you don't have the 15 to 40 minutes that might be necessary to write 200 words. Perhaps you only have about five minutes. Instead of writing free-form, write something more specific like a character description.

Character descriptions work fantastically as notes that will complement your writing in the future. A character description is a list of the attributes of one of the characters in your soon-to-be book. You might write out some of the things your character wears, what the character sounds like and maybe even the life philosophy of the character.

The description does not even need to be something written as it could be a drawing or a collection of items. Regardless of what form your description takes, try to take five minutes to flesh out this character a bit more. Taking this time may lead to a flurry of ideas later on when you've scheduled out an hour of writing time at night or over the weekend.

Feel free to print out your character descriptions (or type them up and then print them out) and to place them around the work station you've created for yourself at home.


## Afternoon Activity #3: Get the Blood Moving

The brain works better when there is oxygen flowing its way. This is why the potential morning activity of exercising is so important. You will think better and more creatively if your brain has the energy and oxygen it needs. If you are having problems writing 200 words or a character description due to writer's block, you may need to go for a little walk.

Taking 10 minutes during your lunch break to walk around the block or up and down the stairs may seem a bit silly but it can increase your energy levels for the entire afternoon. Since you'll more than likely be sitting the rest of the day, it is important to take the opportunity to keep your circulation going.

Of course, there are many added benefits to supplementing your day with exercise. It may help you to lose weight and improve your cardiovascular endurance. Exercise is a fantastic social opportunity as you may be able to find a walking buddy to keep you motivated. If you're going outside, this also gives you a chance to absorb a little bit of sun which is great for your mood and your accumulation of vitamin D.

Even if you didn't have the chance to write during your lunches and you took the time to get a tiny walk in, I believe it would still end up helping your writing in the long run. The added evening energy alone will work wonders on your productivity.

## Afternoon Activity #4: Research, Research, Research

There are many different kinds of books that you could be writing. If you are writing an imaginative fiction book that depends more on character descriptions and plot points than research, you might be able to write most of it from memory on the fly. For most other types of books, you will have to perform some degree of research.

This is one of the things that hold people back from creating their work in the first place. For instance, if you wanted to write a fiction work set in the 1930's in New York City, you might have to research what clothes your characters would wear, some of the areas they might live in and what general life was like during that time. It could be hours and hours worth of research that you never see yourself accomplishing.

This is a perfect activity to accomplish during your lunch hour. There are plenty of employees that use this time to surf the Web regardless, so you may as well do some background work on your book. Be prepared for this, by putting some bookmarks to research sites on your Internet Favorites and take out a few pertinent books from the library that will aid you in your quest.

If you take care of all this research now, it will be much easier to sit down and actually write when you have a few hours to spare in the evening or on the weekend. If you are using the Internet for this research try not to get distracted by the time-sucking practices of link clicking, social media use and e-mail checking.

## Afternoon Activity #5: Stretch Armstrong

I will admit that this is a silly activity that is a tiny bit awkward. Regardless, I have tried it on multiple occasions and it always leaves me feeling fresh and ready for the second half of the day. The activity is to use the last five minutes of your lunch break to do a full-out stretch routine. While the perfect place for this sort of thing would be at a gym (if you have a gym at your office, take advantage of it), many offices do not offer such amenities. I have found that the second best place for it, oddly enough, is the bathroom.

Now, since a full stretch routine takes up a large amount of space, it is best to use a bathroom on a different, less-traveled floor than your own, or one of those family bathrooms in which you can lock the door entirely. If this activity isn't silly enough, I usually remove my pants while stretching to ensure I don't split them when I try to touch my toes.

I understand that standing in a family bathroom with your pants off trying to do a stretch routine is kind of weird. But if you have the door locked, nobody is going to see you and you can focus on the wonderful benefits.

Stretching is a key for total body health and it is another activity that improves the circulation and thus the flow of oxygen to the brain. I stretch for about five minutes at a time, focusing mostly on my legs and back. I pretty much use the same stretch routine I led as a wrestling team captain back in high school as it leaves me feeling limber and energized.

Whichever of these five activities you decide to do, you will either have made progress on your book or you will have improved your chances for progress later by increasing your energy. Try all of them (even the stretching) at least once to see which one works for you the best in your particular lunch situation.


## Plan Adjustment/Notes

At the end of your lunch break or right when you come back you should make any changes necessary in the plan you formed earlier in the day. You may have received an e-mail that will require an adjustment in your evening, or an impromptu meeting could have been scheduled that will affect your afternoon. Plans are meant to be edited, altered, and improved upon, so don't worry about having to spruce them up a bit. If reality always reflected our plans, we would get bored pretty quickly.

Also, if any of the notes you've taken on your note pad have filled you with excitement, take this time to further brainstorm off of them. This can really set you on a tangent mentally, so make sure to actually return to work...unless you want to be a full-time writer, then leave a nice note and head out the door.

## Side Note: Triage

One of my favorite analogies I've read about prioritization during your day compared your daily goals and tasks to triage. In an article on his website, Steve Pavlina states that picking and choosing the objectives for your day are somewhat like the morbid task of a person working triage in a hospital. During an intense crisis, in which there are people who might not survive, a doctor must act quickly deciding how to classify an incoming patient if there are only so many doctors to go around.

A patient who is unlikely to survive is classified differently than a patient who will survive but only with intense care. These patients are classified differently than patients who will survive with or without care.

This is a very intense comparison, but from time to time you must be just as ruthless with your life. There are often not enough hours in the day to get everything done. It can be difficult to determine which things should make the cut. Use the theory of triage but connect it to the goals you have chosen for yourself.

Take an item from your to-do list or plan for the day. Ask yourself, "Is this task necessary for me to do today to complete my goals?" If it is, put some kind of symbol next to it indicating its importance. If not, ask yourself "Will this task contribute in some way to me completing my goals?" If so, mark it with another symbol. If not, the item is not important toward completing your goals and thusly it is lowered in priority.

These lower priority items must be removed from your to-do list to make way for the more important tasks. If you make silly things like checking your e-mail 100 times a day or looking up the latest in celebrity gossip a priority, your goals and fulfillment will fall by the wayside.

Now, there are certain things you need to do regardless, like picking up your kids from soccer practice and filing your taxes before a certain date. These are probably priority one regardless (since being a good parent and a lawful citizen are most certainly goals of yours) and will require that you spend a certain amount of time on them.

Nobody said that becoming a writer was going to be easy. There are some things that you may have to drop from your life to make time for your desired side-career. But if you do, you have the chance to join the part of the population that is actually making a run for some life-affirming goals. This is a victory that is far superior to winning celebrity trivia night and some free appetizers at your local watering hole.

## Breathing

You are back to work and nearing the 2 PM hour. At this time you may feel a little sluggishness, some of which is brought on by the food, some is a result of your body's natural clock, but some might be because you're sitting down and not all of the energy is flowing properly. Take some time at 2 PM to just breathe.

I realize that we already sort of covered this in the Take a Moment section, but this goes to show how important breathing is to your performance and creativity. If the oxygen continues the flow in the proper way, hopefully your energy and creativity will as well.

Take in your surroundings, stop what you're doing, breathe in a big deep breath and take a big deep breath out. Repeat this a few times. For some people who are not used to breathing for this purpose (breathing just to breathe), there is a big change that can come over them. They feel more awake, more alive and more focused on the tasks ahead of them. Incorporate this step into your afternoon and it will help keep the balloon bouncing just a little bit longer.

Personally, I noticed a little while ago that any time that I was angry, upset, or feeling bad about myself; this was directly connected to my breath. It was almost as if logic was in direct proportion to my breathing. If I wasn't breathing well, I wasn't thinking clearly about my emotional state. If I was breathing, I could overcome my negative thoughts and work my way back to being happy.

If this holds true for even a fraction of the population, I have definitely seen a few people who could stand to take a breath or three. Are you one of them? Take this breathing time seriously and it could change your life for the better.

## Mid-Afternoon: 2 PM to 4 PM

## Hydration

Another one of those "reasons we get tired that we don't quite realize at the time" is dehydration. While we're sitting there typing away we sometimes get so focused in on the work that we don't take into account how much water we've had. When I used to work in an office more regularly, I could never quite explain my 2:30 PM lull. I would eat an energy bar and try to take a walk around. I'd even have a 2nd or 3rd cup of coffee (I hadn't weaned myself off of that stuff yet) and still I felt dead in the water.

The coffee, the food, the sitting, the walking, and the typing was all keeping me from drinking more water than the typically tiny cups that are provided at offices. This is also another anti-coffee and caffeine notice: these products are diuretics which make you lose water faster. All this lack of drinking and water loss can lead to you feeling agitated and spacey. The way to get this back is to take a big long drink at the water fountain or to fill a few big cups with water and drink them over the next hour or so. You may need to use the restroom more often than usual later, but your brain will thank you for the support.

Recent theories in the personal development field have also connected water with emotion. In the movie, *What the Bleep Do We*

*Know?*, scientists showed that water that had been sent positive thoughts took on a more crystalline and ordered pattern. Water that had been sent negative thoughts looked downright ugly under a microscope. This is completely strange, but maybe there is something to it.

Humans are over 60% water living in a world covered in up to 70% water. Even if this theory is purely psychological, it may be worth sending some positivity your water's way before you drink it.


## Plant a Seed

This is the step that is a bit of preparation for later in the day and it is decidedly optional. One of the things that helps me get through the day is knowing that I have people I could call who would say nice things to me. If I'm ever feeling down, I call one of them up and try to move the conversation toward me getting a compliment and feeling better about myself. If you have a person like that in your life, send them a nice text around 3 PM or so. Just a "happy to have you in my life" or a "miss you, was thinking of you" text.

This is a win-win situation. You have the knowledge of sending a really nice text to someone that you can refer back to from your Sent box for the rest of the day. You can feel good about brightening up your friend's time at work. If you receive a text back, wait until the end of work to check it. When you do, chances are that it will be another nice and positive text waiting to lift your spirits. The only catch of this is that you should really feel the feelings that you send in the first text message so you don't feel like a fraud when you receive the reply. If you are being truthful, both sending and receiving these positive texts will make everything feel just a little bit better.


## A Minute Away

One of my favorite tricks at work to keep myself fresh has always been to take a little trip to the bathroom or a walk around to make sure that my eyes hadn't been burned out by the screen. A minute here and there can make a major difference in your day. A couple of these ideas fall into the "weird" category, but as I said earlier, it always helps to have a bit of faith when keeping yourself motivated.

## One Minute Activity #1: Smile and Laugh

One of the major reasons that I like to emphasize breathing in this book is because it is a fantastic reliever of tension. We hold so much tension throughout the day whether it's our negative feelings, or worries or our natural tendency. A little tip I learned in acting class from my own personal guru, Joan Darling, also applies quite well in life.

When I was doing a scene in acting class with a partner, Joan would occasionally give us notes from the side during the action. One of her favorite quotes was the phrase, "Let yourself laugh." After hearing it, my partner and I would both exhale with a chuckle. Whenever I let myself do that, I would always feel lighter as if a great deal of tension had been lifted. For some reason, it never interfered with the acting in a bad way; it actually made things more natural and real.

This tip works wonders in the real world as well. If you have a minute alone and you catch yourself holding on to a negative feeling or emotion or you just feel a bit stuffed up with work activities, try letting yourself laugh. In addition, smiling and laughing are thought to be extremely healthy and it never hurts to put more of a healthy activity into your day.

## One Minute Activity #2: A Little Love

Chalk this up as one of the weird ideas that work. I've used this to my own benefit and I thoroughly recommend it.

Either go into the restroom or take out a pocket mirror of some kind. Check around to make sure that nobody is in the room or within earshot. Look at yourself and think of at least three things that are positive about you. Say the phrase, "I love you because," and then fill in the blanks with those three positive traits. Then finish it off by just saying, "I love you."

This exercise was devised by one of the masters of self-esteem, Jack Canfield of the *Chicken Soup for the Soul* series. It provokes a reaction similar to the Smile and Laugh activity. It removes a burden and it makes you feel warm inside. During the middle of a tough work day, it can be awesome to get a little bit of love, even if it's from a mirror image of yourself.

If you are worried about dropping the "L" bomb to yourself, try replacing the phrase "I love you" with something like "You are awesome." Whatever floats your boat!

## One Minute Activity #3: A Positive Encounter

While planting a seed for a later compliment is nice, there's nothing like getting the milk straight from the cow. By that of course I mean talking to one of your co-workers and having a positive little chat. Many conversations with co-workers take on the form of an "us vs. them" mentality, in which bosses and requirements are critiqued.

Unfortunately, going negative with these conversations, while making you feel pumped up with solidarity for a bit, is not helpful in the long run. Instead, try talking about something positive or saying that you think the other person did a great job with something. Expressing appreciation is much more uplifting than expressing discontent. You picked the job and it is paying you. You are in much better shape than a lot of unemployed people in the world right now. Count your blessings and stay positive.

Adding a ritual like a conversation of appreciation to your work day will help you feel fresh and motivated. A state that will benefit your writing considerably if you have some time scheduled for the task later in the evening.

## One Minute Activity #4: The Sedona Method

Taking a one minute break in the afternoon is best when you are having an emotional issue or blockage during your day. When I felt low and down on myself during my 9 to 5 job in the "What am I doing with my life?" sort of way, I wish that I'd had a solution like The Sedona Method to help me through it.

A man named Lester Levenson in his 40s was having major health problems and doctors believed the end was near. He used a new healing method that involved letting go of his painful thoughts to improve his health and live another four decades. Levenson follower Hale Dwoskin picked up the method after Levenson's death and it has become a phenomenon in the self-help circle in both print and film.

The method consists of three questions that deal with your current feelings. Focus on a negative feeling or emotion you might be having, like distaste with your last few hours of work. First you ask yourself, "Could I release this feeling?" Answer the question in your mind and then ask, "Would I release this feeling if I could?" Answer that question and then ask, "When?" Even if your answers are "No, no, and never," you will almost certainly feel a release of some of these negative and frustrating emotions.

The questions work either out loud or in your head. Try to visualize your feelings as a pencil that you're gripping onto with your hand. The feelings aren't a part of you, you're simply holding onto them tightly. When you do this exercise, it's like dropping the pencil on the ground. You are able to let go of the feelings completely because you aren't your feelings.

## One Minute Activity #5: Get a Little Air

In the old days, getting a little air was relegated to smokers. Now that smoking has fallen off a bit due to health concerns and tougher economic times, going outside and breathing in some fresh oxygen is much more possible.

I have found this to make a major difference, especially when working in a particularly stuffy office (or in my similarly stuffy apartment). Getting some air and some sun can really change the outlook of your day in a hurry.

If you are alone outside, you can complete three of the four other exercises. This is a particularly positive routine that I fully endorse during your minute away from the madness.

## Late Afternoon: 4 PM to 6 PM

### Staying Late

Repeat any of the previous steps between 4 PM and 5 PM if you need a little boost of energy. A smart snack or a stretch can do wonders if you're getting sleepy. When 5 PM rolls around there is a big feeling of joy as you can finally get home and start working on the "fun stuff." Hold on. Let's make sure we know what we're doing first.

Remember when the bell would ring for the end of class in high school? Most of the kids quickly packed up their stuff and ran to get a conversation or two in before the next class. Some of the kids slowly organized their things and took a look at what was coming up. That is what you should do before you go home.

Take another look at your plan and make sure you know what's going to happen next. Jot down any last second thoughts that will help you out. Gather a little bit of excitement for the productivity you're about to work with. Use a moment or two to visualize yourself writing. Look at the goals that you've placed for yourself around your office and in your wallet. Once you've done all of that, you can make the trek back home.

### Unwanted Calls/Tasks

It's time to get back on the train or into the car. Before you throw on that amazing audio program you were listening to earlier, you should take some time to get the unwanted tasks out of the way. Did your wife ask you to pick something up? Go to a grocery store before you start the trek home. Was there a pressing message left on your machine while you were at work? Give them a quick call before you get in the car or while you're on the train.

Taking care of these things now ensures fewer distractions when you sit down and start to work at home or at the place of your choosing. There is no bigger buzz kill then getting into your creative flow and having someone tell you that there is an immediate problem that needs to be addressed. Nip it in the butt and take care of that sort of stuff right now.

## Side Note: Protect Your Time

Often, this late afternoon, early evening period is the time that has presented me with the most plan-derailing monkey wrenches. I would be asked to take an evening phone call right in the middle of my writing plans or I'd be asked to go to a dinner that would cut my writing time down from an hour to 10 minutes. These are the sorts of things that can bust up your writing plans before they start.

Try your best to protect your writing time as if it is the most important thing in your day. Imagine that your writing date with yourself is like a business meeting that has been inked into your planner for weeks. If you miss a few writing days in a row, it ceases to be a habit anymore. Keeping the habit going strong allows you to use less will power. The less energy you need to put into forcing yourself to write, the better chance you have of getting work on your book completed.

Get used to telling people that you're busy and you can't help out with things. I've missed out on some fun nights out and some interesting opportunities, but I'm proud of myself for sticking to my guns and keeping everyday writing a part of my life.

## Learning 2: The Revenge

Once those dreaded tasks are out of the way, feel free to go back to your audio listening. If you feel like you weren't able to quite absorb the information from earlier in the program, rewind it back and listen to it again. There are so many tidbits of life advice out there that you might as well try to get them all while you're taking the time out of your day.

Here's one suggestion to make any kind of personal development stick which I learned from Steven Covey. Make the effort to teach the info you pick up almost immediately to someone else. This will help you to get a well-rounded understanding of the concept.

If you talk about these newly learned concepts with your friends and family, they are likely to bring it up with you again. It has been amazing being able to discuss happiness with my girlfriend, my friends and my parents. Telling them the things I've learned has led to many discussions on the subject that never would have occurred had I kept these tidbits of wisdom to myself. This further reinforces the learning, making sure that I keep my happiness and health in the forefront of my mind.

## Conclusion

You are amazing! You have gone from 6 AM to 6 PM and you are still happy and motivated as you walk in through the front door. This is when the typical American Leisure Time kicks in. You will be spending your time a little bit differently than the masses.

If you have trouble with any particular part of this afternoon daily motivation, don't worry. You do not have to be perfect for it to have an effect. It will get easier over time and you will become a stronger more motivated person. Keep plugging away. Your co-workers might even ask you how you've made such a change. Just tell them a little bird gave you a few ideas.

# 5 THE EVENING

You have put in a full day of work after getting a bit of writing done in the morning. Your energy is at a pretty good level due to Smart Snacks, Breathing and Stretching. The societal instinct is to settle in with a hefty cooked dinner and some television. The creative person, however, needs to use this time to work on his craft. Writing in the evening on your workdays serves as great weekly motivation. You won't just be an employee for five days in a row; you will be a writer throughout the entire week.

This is also the time that your friends will ask you to come out and hang/drink. There is no problem doing this every so often, but if you go out and drink every night it can seriously cut into your writing time. Try these tactics a couple of times to start out. I suspect that if you get that burst of motivation from writing after work every so often, you will want to experience it more and more. It might even be more fun than your typical nighttime beer guzzling.

## Early Evening: 6 PM to 8 PM

### Take Care of Business

You have arrived home via car, train or bus. What is the first thing that typically happens when you get home? Either your apartment/house or the person you live with begins to ask you to do things. If it's just the apartment/house this request can come in the form of a dirty pile of clothes on the floor or a sink full of dirty dishes. If it's someone you live with, then they are telling you about these clothes or dishes or asking you to help them with a project. Personally this has taken the wind out of my sails many a time.

Give yourself a half hour to an hour to take care of business. Get those clothes into a hamper, wash those dishes, and help out your roommate. Be very clear to yourself and that person that you only have a limited amount of time, but do not complain or have a pity party about these tasks. There is no reason to bring any negative energy into the situation. Be happy to step in and help and if you aren't happy, fake it until you make it. By getting these things out of the way before getting into any writing at all, you can feel accomplished and knock out a lot of potential distractions for the rest of the evening.

If there are too many tasks that need your attention, you have two options. You can limit yourself to an hour of work on them and then head off to another location to get your writing done. This step will probably lead to you spending a whole hour on these activities every evening. Unless your apartment/house is a complete disaster, an hour a day is bound to clear up even the worst of problems within a week or two. The second option is to spend the whole evening, and any successive evenings, completely eradicating the problem. You won't get any writing done, but at least you will no longer have this looming requirement hanging over your head.

## Dinner

This is not the time to pig out. If you make dinner your largest meal of the day as most people do, you will become sleepy for the rest of the night. Be sensible. Figure out some dishes that are easy to prepare and that are light in nature. If you go out to eat, get something with a lot of vegetables that isn't completely covered in cheese or sauce. The important thing, as it is with the other meals of the day, is that you are using this meal to gain energy not to take it away. By eating too much food that is cooked heavily or deep fried, your energy will be spent trying to break down that food in your stomach. That means less energy for your brain and your writing.

Be healthy in your dinner and you will be smarter in the evening.


## Side Note: Eating Out

Let's say that your normal healthy dinner plan is thwarted by a trip out with your friends to a restaurant. If you're like I am, your first instinct is to buy a big juicy hamburger slathered in barbecue sauce or a giant plate of pasta. If you have any writing time scheduled for after the meal, those two gargantuan dinners will keep your brain slow and your energy low. When you eat a big meal, all the oxygen and all the energy goes into trying to digest the sucker.

Obviously, I want you to be able to enjoy yourself, but I'm simply trying to protect any writing time that you might have afterward. Here are a few tips to keep your energy and creativity up.

You should take advantage of tip-hungry waiters and drink as much water as possible (you should also tip these tip-hungry waiters well). Water will aid in your digestion and it will help to fill you up so you don't need to eat as much. Skip the wine or beer if you know you'll be writing later. Personally, even one or two drinks will have a major effect on me and my writing. The second that I sit down and try to focus I feel like taking a nap after a few drinks.

Be like Meg Ryan in *When Harry Met Sally* and customize your order. Get dressing on the side, especially if you're ordering a big salad. While some dressings are high in healthy fats, others are loaded with saturated fats that will put you to sleep and work a number on your digestion. Choose the healthiest side dishes like the house salad or fresh vegetables. Fries and tater tots are often loaded with sleep-inducing cooked oil.

Skip dessert if possible or share the dessert with a couple of people. Dessert is just a sugar high (and subsequent sugar crash) waiting to happen, which is awesome if you're headed straight home to bed and it sucks if you're trying to work on your novel. Just wolf down another glass of water and get ready to write!

## Preparation

Now it's time to get organized. Set up your writing space just the way you like it. Gather all of your materials: pens, pencils, research sources, a cup of water, desk lamp, comfortable chair, quiet space, etc. This should take you 10 to 15 minutes to get things exactly the way you want them, if you are an OCD person like me. Normal people can probably accomplish this task in five minutes or so.

An organized space can help you get your thoughts out. There are fewer distractions and you can feel more professional. If there are things missing from your workspace that will take too long for you to get this evening, try to deal without them for tonight and put getting that item on your to-do list for the next day. I'm sure you'll do OK without your lucky writing bear just for one night.

## Side Note: Removing Distractions

If you have chosen a writing space at home, you may face an uphill battle to push past the many possible distractions you can run into. I have some friends, like my brilliant mathematician, musician pal from down the street, who are able to deal with a hurricane and a party in the next room while continuing to do work. I on the other hand, could see a bright, shiny object and be thrown off for hours.

Here are the five top distractions that you could face at home and how to take care of them swiftly.

## Home Distraction #1: Electronic Noise Machines

The first distraction is often some kind of device like the phone, television or computer making noise in the form of a text, show or instant message. The simplest way to deal with this distraction is to turn the item off. I find that I am at least twice as productive when I turn my cell phone off. It's like turning off the constant thought in the back of my mind that someone might call to distract me. If someone in your house is watching television, ask them to turn the volume way down or you could put on some noise cancelling headphones. If you are using the computer to write, turn off all communication programs and unplug the Internet completely.

In essence, put yourself on an island of writing. Make it so nobody can get in touch with you and nobody can bother you.


## Home Distraction #2: Growing To-Do List

If you live with a significant other like I do, you probably know the feeling of the growing to-do list. A list of three things that you take care of earlier in the evening can grow to 10 items by the end of it. It is also possible that saying, "But I'm working on my writing," can earn you a scowl and a trip to the couch if you don't say it the right way.

One of the best ways to deal with this situation is the trade-off. Trade one task for another, stating that you'll take care of a task the other person usually does in trade for tasks on your to-do list tonight. Another option is to wait until after your writing is completed to take care of the tasks. If you have any other people living in the house (like kids or roommates) perhaps you can delegate the task to them as well.

If you do not live with someone and your to-do list is still growing, try to take care of the most urgent items quickly and efficiently with a positive attitude. Get a reasonable amount of it completed and then lock the to-do list out for a little while until you get some writing completed.


## Home Distraction #3: Hungry, Thirsty and Tired

It's a strange psychological phenomenon, but when we are in the comfort zone of our apartment or home, we tend to want to be hyper-satisfied. I know that if I'm out at a coffee shop and I'm a little bit hungry, I might be willing to hold off because I know that their list is short on healthy items and I have to shell out some money to get them. If I'm at home, it won't take much to get me distracted enough to get up for a snack.

If you keep your area stocked with some healthy snacks and water, you can keep yourself from getting too distracted with these life essentials. Leaving yourself a natural protein bar or two and some baggies of raw almonds along with a bottle or two of chilled water can work wonders. Having these items near your side might keep you from a time-consuming trip to the refrigerator, which will put you in line of to-do list requests, television distractions and all sorts of other stuff.

Consider your writing area like your little bomb shelter against distractions. Keep yourself stocked to survive.

## Home Distraction #4: Lack of Motivation

In high school, I was an all-star of productivity. When I hit college, home became a place to relax and avoid all work whatsoever. I'm not sure why that came to be, but I do know that the solution involves getting motivated.

I've mentioned methods like keeping positive, listening to inspirational audio programs and reading motivating quotes earlier and all those still apply. The main thing to get over at home is that you might be trained not to do any work there. This is the brain, which loves its habits, asserting authority again. The more you get used to working at home, the fewer problems you will have getting motivated.

I know, I know, this sounds like the conundrum that you need experience in a job you can't seem to get without experience in that job. Trust me though, if you practice motivation and you practice writing at home, you will eventually be able to build up your tolerance to demons like procrastination and low self-esteem.

## Home Distraction #5: Not Enough Room

This is a problem I have run into in a few of my, less spacious choices of living. There are two options for this problem. Either work somewhere outside of your home or carve out a little area for yourself and hope for the best.

There are many ways to work outside of the home if you have a laptop and a Wi-Fi connection and there are even more ways to write if you have a few sheets of paper and a pencil. Almost all of these methods, aside from a public library will cost you money. Coffee shops with Internet tend to be the best bang for your buck as you can get some tea, a hot chocolate or a scone to accompany you in your writing. Another option is to rent out writing spaces that are available in some cities. Authors essentially rent out a cubicle that they pay for monthly.

Setting up a tiny writing area (or multiple tiny writing areas) in your tiny apartment is imperative if you plan to write at home. Put some notes and motivational quotes up in a corner, clear off some desk space and try your best to be closed off from the rest of the apartment.

Since some of my Chicago apartments have been too small, writing elsewhere became a necessity. Do whatever you feel is necessary to get your work done either domestically or (slightly) abroad.

## Mid-Evening: 8 PM to 10 PM

## Write

It's your time to shine! Work on your current project or a project you've been meaning to but putting off. You can draw from your morning plan or start something new. All your daily motivation has been leading up to this and the door is open and ready for you to write. So do it!

If you don't know what to write, check out some writing prompts. You can visit my website, Build Creative Writing Ideas for hundreds of them. If you don't like these story starters, simply start writing something, anything. Eventually what you write will turn into an idea or a project and you can go from there. It is up to you how long you want to write, but if possible write for the entire two hours.

When a writer is first starting out, it can be tough for him or her to write for more than a few minutes at a time. Over time, you can train yourself to do better. You may even feel compelled to write all day long on a Saturday or Sunday. Until you get that comfortable though, you might feel stuck in the early going. Persevere and try to do just a little bit more every day.

## A Treat

If you lose your motivation a bit or you get hungry/tired, try giving yourself a treat. I often use food to treat myself, like a fresh, juicy apple or some kettle corn. Food works for me due to the quick energy boost and the good feelings associated with eating something sweet and tasty. Once again, try not to go overboard with how much you eat and what you eat.

The treat does not have to be food. It should still be somewhat healthy, not too lengthy, and make you feel good. Some examples are a quick walk outside, a phone call to a good friend, and watching an entertaining webisode on the Internet. Don't use the treat to tangent off and quit writing for the night. Use the treat to push you forward into as much writing as possible.

## Change Location

It is difficult to avoid the distractions of the home. If you are starting to lose steam or you feel the pull of other tasks in the house, change locations. Go to a coffee shop or a diner or a library or anywhere that is open for at least the next hour or two that you think you will be able to write in. Often, a simple change in space can bring new energy to your writing and give you an extra hour of motivation without doing anything too drastic.

This optional step also gives you a great deal to draw from if you aren't sure of what to write. You can people watch and describe the new location to your heart's content.

Changing to a new location is a trick to keep that motivation balloon bouncing in the air one last time. More often than not it will work and sometimes it will not. Stay at this new location as long as you wish and when you are tired or feel unmotivated return home. There is a chance that even being in this other place for a short period of time will recharge you when you get back.

## Late Evening: 10 PM to 12 AM

### Last Call

It's getting late (for some) and your eyes are getting heavy. You may have been fired up with inspiration and your pen scribbled furiously just an hour earlier, but now you are starting to drag.

Get your last few ideas down on paper. It can help to outline the next few sections of what you were writing in a very basic format. This way you don't feel as though you will miss out on the great brainstorms you had this evening, you can pick right back up tomorrow. There is a chance that one of your great ideas will hit now as you're getting sleepy. The relaxation of sleepiness can allow brilliant thoughts when there isn't so much tension or pressure. Of course, you should write these down and flesh them out tomorrow.

### Organize

Put all of your writing and materials back in a place where you can easily find them tomorrow. If you leave your area organized now, you will need to do less preparation for the next evening's session.

Begin to prepare for your next work day. Iron clothes, prepare lunches, and do any other tasks that will help you be ready for the following morning. If you do not have to do a whole lot to get ready for tomorrow, take on one aspect of your general organization that needs fixing. Deconstruct an old filing system that no longer functions, go through some old mail and throw out all the junk, or condense two drawers of junk into one drawer of junk. If you continue to knock down some of these old organizational blocks, over time you will become a lot more put together.

## Side Note: Healthy Bedtime Routine

As a morning person, I have found it difficult from time to time to plan out a healthy bedtime routine. I would often throw my clothes in a large pile, leave my desk a mess and just crash into bed. I know now that this just ends up placing a burden on my morning. If I don't get to my evening mess for a couple of mornings in a row, I can feel easily overwhelmed by the tasks that I've created to distract myself.

Take a minute or two to walk through your place and tidy up. Throw out things that need tossing and put items you've taken out back into their rightful places. If you have time, set aside some clothes for yourself for the morning so that upon waking you can focus on the day ahead. Imagine that the evening version of you is like a house guest of the morning person. Treat the morning person's house with respect and make it as tidy as possible.

Perhaps the morning person will reward you with some amazing brainstorms to write from the following evening!

## Recharge

It is time for bed and the opportunity to recharge for the next day of daily motivation. If you have gotten through all of these crazy motivational steps throughout the day, you are probably feeling pretty damn good about yourself. Remember that as you lie down to sleep. Tomorrow is a day in which you can do exactly the same if not even better.

Just as you did during work, keep a notepad beside your bed when you are going to sleep. As I stated earlier, the relaxation you feel as you are drifting away can lead to a great idea coming to the front of your mind. Don't worry if it takes you a little longer to sleep than usual. Surprisingly, getting more things done can give you more energy at the end of the day. Relax or read a book to help you to convince your brain it's time to sleep. Sweet dreams.

## Conclusion

Getting through an entire work day with a good deal of motivation and productivity is not easy. Staying motivated to write for most of the day is good enough and it is still probably better than most of the working population. If you find this too overwhelming, take it one step at a time, one day at a time. You don't have to be perfect but you do have to be a writer. The only thing stopping you is you. So write already!

# 6 THE WEEKEND

If you've made it through an entire week of brainstorming, writing and motivation, you may be especially excited to have some time to sit down and make your writing happen at long length. The weekend is a time in which you can make some very positive progress because you may be able to set aside an entire half-day or full-day simply for writing.

Many of the tips that I've already mentioned completely apply to your weekend writing as well. There are a few key things to keep in mind though, as different distractions and challenges can come up now that you're away from your desk.

This window of time (especially the morning) is in the running for the most productive time of the week. There are a few hours during this period that your significant other and kids are asleep, which as much as you may love them, leads to a distraction free existence for a bit. If you don't have to go into work that day, there are few job-related problems cropping up, and even if there were, there's no need to deal with them while nobody but you is awake. People, this is your time to shine.

Since the weekend tends to be more of a free-flowing time, I won't break things down to every two hours in this section. Instead, for the weekend, I will give you my Golden 10 Tips for the Weekend. Employ as many or as few as you wish to help you in your weekend writing journey.

## Golden Tip #1: Wake Up Early

If you are early to bed on Friday and/or Saturday night and early to rise the next day, you will have a much more productive weekend as a whole. Giving yourself a couple of extra hours without distraction can work wonders. I have used the early weekend wake-up to write an entire screenplay in a day, to finish off my non-fiction books and in high school, I even used it as my SAT prep time.

Don't be too worried about being lame on a weekend night every so often. I promise you that your friends will think you are much less lame once you have a book to your credit.

Adding an early morning wake-up to your weekend also has an added effect. It will make it much easier for you to wake up early during the week. After a bit of time, you will no longer feel the need for as many snooze alarms or lattes. You will be awake naturally because your brain is used to it.

## Golden Tip #2: Cement Your Purpose

The weekend is fantastic because you have the potential free time to do so much in your writing. It is also dangerous, because all this free time can make you lazy. I've had more than one weekend that I'd planned on making productive spin out of control due to a lack of focus.

If you cement your purpose early on in the day, you are less likely to have a lack of concentration. Use the goal and purpose exercises from earlier in the book to create an objective or two for yourself. Write them out on a sheet of paper and read them out loud to yourself before you do anything on Saturday or Sunday.

While this is a smart idea for any day of the week, it is especially important when you have the freedom of choice during the weekend. Reading these out loud in the morning gives you a voice in the back of your head that says, "there is a bigger purpose behind my life." Imagine that voice chiming in when you are invited to watch several hours of bad reality television or the latest blow-them-up action flick. A strong purpose pushes your choices in the direction of your writing.

## Golden Tip #3: Far, Far Away

As I fought against procrastination after my college years, I figured out that my desires to avoid work ran deep at that time. Even if I went to a coffee shop around the corner, my brain could not be tricked. It knew that a giant burst of fear or discomfort would send me right back in front of the television at my apartment.

To make sure that I was focused when I was away from the apartment, I tried to cut off my lines of escape. Instead of a short walk away from procrastination, I made sure that I was at least a solid mile. I would take the train at least several stops away to a coffee shop. This is one of the best parts about having a laptop; the ability to do work anywhere. And so anywhere is where I did it.

I began to "strand" myself at coffee shops in parts of town I'd never been to. It was like my anti-procrastination tour. Obviously, when I was out I'd have to spend a few bucks on a snack and a couple on the train or bus ride, but it was worth it to make sure I got some time in.

This plan worked for me because I had to pause before considering a return to my apartment. When I was so close to home it was easy for my procrastination to convince me to head back. When I was farther away, convincing myself to go back after I'd come all the way out there to work was much tougher. I have gotten so much work finished using this method, in so many different places, I could probably lead a tour of the city's best coffee shops. Perhaps I should do that if the writing career doesn't pan out.

## Golden Tip #4: Just Start Writing

One of my favorite improvisational comedy classes I've ever taken was at the Annoyance Theater in Chicago. They trained me to get out of my head and start talking immediately during a scene. This prevented the sometimes awkward beginnings of a comedy scene where neither performer really knows what he or she is doing. Learning this scene-starting technique has helped me past multiple cases of writer's block in my life.

Stop me if your typical writing routine sounds like the following: you sit down to write on your laptop but before you start to check your e-mail. You supplement your e-mail window with one or two news websites and a YouTube video that your friend has showed you. After the video, you write down a note or two about something you need to do later in the day. Before you know it, 15 minutes have passed and you have done no writing whatsoever.

This is why you need to start writing immediately. To get those 15 minutes back; to claim them for your creativity instead of for the boring stuff that everybody else does with his or her time. Put pen to paper or hand to keyboard and force the words out of your brain. They might not be perfect but at the least you are building up some momentum. Starting, continuing and finishing a book is all about momentum.

By starting to write as soon as you sit down, you save time, build up momentum and improve your level of writing confidence. It took a long time, but I now truly feel that at any point, anywhere and at any time of the day, I can start writing if I need to. Once you leap that hurdle, writing becomes a whole lot easier.

## Golden Tip #5: The Back-Up Plan

I feel like sometimes, writers like me who tell you how to change your life for the better come off as if they have no flaws whatsoever. For instance, since I'm telling you about writing I must have completely defeated procrastination forever and I have it all figured out. While I have gathered a lot of tips and tricks over the years, I'm certainly not immune to writer's block and I can cite at least twice over the last week where I had to resort to a back-up plan to finish my writing for the day.

There is no telling what is going to trigger writer's block and where it's going to occur. You might have a perfectly logical plan of locking yourself in your room and writing for several hours. You might have some water handy and a few snacks here and there. You may have repeated your purpose out loud so many times that you're hoarse. And yet, despite all that, you might have trouble writing word one for your story that day.

This doesn't mean anything is wrong with you; it's just the way it goes sometimes. The best way to counteract this problem is to have a back-up plan. For example, today I was planning on getting up at 6:30 a.m. and writing by 7. By 7:45 a.m., I had yet to do anything and I only had a few hours to do my 2,000 words for the day before I had to leave for errands. The original plan was sound, but the flesh and mind just weren't willing. I felt the icy grip of procrastination on my brain saying things like, "Maybe you should skip your writing today, you can pick back up with it tomorrow. Maybe…"

I sat down for a minute in silence thinking about what was really important: me feeling good about procrastinating in the moment or achieving my goals. This was enough to get my butt out of the house and over to my favorite coffee joint. I'm over halfway done a task that I might not have started in the first place because I changed my location.

Location isn't the only thing you are able to change in case your writing goes south for the day. Other ways you can change up your plan include: writing a different book, poem or script than you planned on, starting with a different chapter or scene, or writing a scene or chapter from a different point of view.

Try to have a few back-up plans in mind in case you are thrown off, because you never know when that pesky writer's block could rear its ugly head.


## Golden Tip #6: Take Care of the Brain

During a day's worth of writing or even an hour's worth, you may need to take a break. There are many different things that people will do to try to recharge themselves and a few of them work better than others. I implore you to try to think of how restful a certain activity is from your brain's perspective.

Closing your eyes and thinking of a few calming thoughts, is a nice, little vacation for the brain. Plopping down in front of the television and watching a bunch of colorful images moving at 24 frames per second with sound a blazing, is not. The same is true for looking at a computer monitor, smart phone screen or almost any digital device. Keep it simple for your brain to ensure that when you get back to writing you will be in peak creative form.

## Golden Tip #7: Brilliant Minds Rest

Leonardo da Vinci created many wonderful things during his lifetime. He was creative and he was prolific. He was also an avid napper. He knew the value of resetting his mental clock so that he could come up with his next brilliant idea.

Some people feel like they need to keep pounding out their writing for many, many consecutive hours. After a while, this becomes akin to drawing water from a stone. Do the best you can for as long as you can, but when you can no longer do your best, feel free to take a nap.

I suggest the "power nap" which is around 20 to 25 minutes. If you sleep any longer, you may fall into a deeper sleep (especially if you're a sleep deprived kind of person) which will leave you feeling groggy.

And remember, if anyone who sees you napping says, "I thought you were writing," You can respond, "I'm pulling a da Vinci!"

## Golden Tip #8: Rampage of Appreciation

Writing is not always a smooth and simple process. You could be going along, writing perfectly well and all of a sudden something stops you. This cannot help but be a little frustrating. If you aren't careful, getting pissed off at yourself could cause your emotions to get the best of you, cutting your writing session short.

I feel like the Hollywood portrayal of the creative writer shows a tortured young soul who cynically thinks the world might end the next day. I used to embody that portrait to a certain extent, and I was nowhere near successful. Until I became more optimistic and able to squelch frustration whenever it cropped up, I was a writer who couldn't write.

One way to shoot your optimism through the roof is to try an exercise called the "Rampage of Appreciation" which I learned from the Jerry and Esther Hicks books about the Law of Attraction.

Look around the room and find something that you're grateful for. Go into some detail in your head about why you appreciate it and why it's important to you. Continue to look through the room to find more objects you appreciate. Now look inside to your feelings and memories and look for things that you appreciate. Try to rattle off every possible positive detail about these items.

Keep this up until you feel positive again. Once you've practiced it a few times, you'll start feeling better immediately when you begin the exercise. This is because you've carved a mental path to appreciation. Not a bad path to take every so often.

## Golden Tip #9: Power in Numbers

If you are having trouble forcing yourself to write, why not enlist the help of some friends who want to get weekend work completed as well? While I don't have many friends who are attempting to write books, I do have several theatre producers and academic types who need to spend a few hours here and there getting work completed.

Having a few friends working with you at your apartment or at the local coffee shop does a few things. It helps you to feel less alone, during what can tend to be a lonely pursuit. Whenever you look up and see your friends plugging away as well, it validates your choice to be sitting and writing on a weekend. Occasionally, if you and your friends make a plan for after the work, it can give you something to look forward to as well, pushing you to write more effectively.

This method does not work if anybody in your group is a "chatty Cathy" or a "distracting Danny" or anyone else that disrupts your progress. Choose the friends who are actually invested in their work. And make sure not to be the distraction in your group, or you might not be asked back to what can be a very productive endeavor.

## Golden Tip #10: Enjoy Your Life

While I am a big proponent of getting writing completed on the weekend (it's Sunday morning before 7 a.m. that I'm currently writing this paragraph), I am also a fan of having a good time with my friends. Despite all these tips of productivity and using the weekend wisely, I know that having a social life is important as well. Going out and experiencing life with your loved ones is relaxing and important and it will help to clear your mind for the next day of writing.

After being so responsible all day, make sure not to go blotto in the evening. I shy away from crazy, drunken occasions like St. Patrick's Day in which everybody feels the obligation to drink themselves silly. My reasoning is that I'll feel horrible the next day. The hangover and potential illness isn't worth it for me personally because I want to be able to write with a full head of steam the next day.

A fun and interesting little challenge for yourself might be to not get drunk at all until you've finished your first book. You might even find it to be such a boon to your productivity that you end up limiting it until the completion of your second book.

## Conclusion

I've never been much of a writing instructor; I'm more like a motivational writing instructor. You might notice that this section is short on actual writing tips but long on tips that might keep you going. If you need some help in the writing skills department, there are many, many books available on the subject. Just make sure to keep this one around for when you need to push past writer's block.

Like I mentioned earlier in the book, there are so many tips in here that you certainly don't need to try to use them all. Use a few of the weekend Golden Tips to give yourself some added productivity. If some of them don't work for you, try the others on for size. For me, life is a grand experiment in efficiency. Keep testing out different combinations of ideas until you get one that works.

Once you've made it a few months with the weekly and weekend writing tips, you may be coming close to the end of your book. The next chapter is all about what you do once you reach that point and how to publish it so you can officially add the title of "author" to your business card.

# 7 GOING ALL THE WAY

If you are almost finished your first book using some of the motivational techniques discussed in the last few chapters, I applaud your efforts. So few of the people who embark on author-hood actually make it do the finish line. Well, perhaps it's not the finish line, but it's definitely a checkpoint with the end in sight.

At the time of writing this book, the digital publishing world is reaching a record pace that doesn't seem to want to slow down while the paper publishing world is declining thoroughly. This chapter will focus on digital and independent publishing since that is what I have done as an author. If you wish to be published by the "Big 6" as they call them, there are many books available on the subject and I strongly you pick up one of them.

I am also not yet what I would call a master of promotion. If you have a high-paying job with some money to spare, I thoroughly recommend taking out advertisements on the Web for your book, pricing the book as low as possible to build up demand and maybe even hiring a publicist to get additional press. For the rest of us, do what you can to get the word out to your friends and loved ones and send out as many review copies as possible. But ... we're getting ahead of ourselves here. Let's make your book a finished product.

## Smoothing Out the Edges

If writing a book is like running a 26.2 mile marathon, touching the book up to smooth out any rough edges is like the guy at the finish like saying "oh, we're actually running 27.2 miles this year." Which is to say that editing is a tedious but not necessarily long process and that if you don't do it you won't truly be finished.

While your book may be quite long, your best first bet is to read the entire thing out loud to yourself (or to a friend if they'll sit there that long). This process will take care of over half of the syntactical errors and most of the typos. Keep in mind, that even if you've spellchecked a document, you will run into many instances of typing the incorrect but properly spelled word in a given situation. Hearing the book read out loud takes care of those pesky situations.

The next step is to have someone with editing experience look the document over. If you have a close friend who is a freelance editor, you may be able to get a decent rate on the project (plug for Ashley Daoust, adeditorial.com). If not, you will either have to shell out a something over $100 or you'll have to do the project in trade. It stinks to spend money when you're not sure if a product will get you any in return, but it is very important to have your book fully edited and ready to go when you decide to publish it.

Once your book has passed the reading test and the editing test, it's time to give it to a few friends for; you guessed it, "the friend test." If you are worried about what your friends might think, just send it to your more encouraging friends. There is no time for a "negative Nancy" opinion when you're trying to publish your first work. Once it's published, "those people" can tell you all the downbeat things they won't about it.

Make any good changes that your friends suggest and ignore the silly ones. When you've gotten all the feedback possible, give the book one last read through out loud. If it passes this final test, you are ready to self-publish your book on the independent market!

## How to Publish Your Digital Book

There are several different approaches you can take when you publish your book digitally and the most effective way to earn money from your book is to use them all. Author JA Konrath is one of the most successful digital book authors of our time, selling thousands of his thriller books every day and inching closer to a seven-figure income every year. Crazily enough, this is only after two years of having been self-published. One of the reasons (and there are many) he has been so successful is that he is using multiple platforms to distribute his book.

While Amazon Kindle sales have given him the most income, he also has received money from books sold through Amazon's CreateSpace, a service that changes digital books into print versions and through Smashwords, which is a service that sends digital books to many other publishing services like the Apple and Sony eBook stores. Another method for digital book selling is through your own website using a hosting service like e-Junkie to sell the book as a PDF.

For all of these methods, the websites involved have extensive help sections with many Frequently Asked Questions that I won't cover here. I'll give you some of the basics that helped me through the process of publishing and you can refer to those websites specifically for any problems you find yourself running into.

## Side Note: Creating a Cover

When I first embarked upon self-publishing, creating a cover for the book worried me. Fortunately, my girlfriend is a former freelance designer and it was not too difficult to convince her to do it for me. If you do not have anyone living with you who is a digital guru, you have a couple of other options.

There are some eBook cover designing programs that aren't too expensive, though they don't create anything beautiful enough to write home about. You can try to do it yourself using a program like Adobe Photoshop, though if you aren't skilled at the process, it may end up looking disastrous. The most effective and most expensive method is to outsource the project completely.

Go on an eBook selling website and look through the covers. Find a few that both fit your genre and style and see if a simple Web search will get you the name of the designer. Contact the designer directly for a quote on a book cover. This can run you over $200 (sometimes over $500) but a fantastic cover can go a long way to selling your book for you. Let the designer know which sites you plan on submitting the book to so that he or she can give you the most appropriately formatted file.

## Amazon Kindle

While I was at first very confused by the submission process to Amazon, it's actually quite simple once you stumble through it a few times. Simply go through your document and change all of your chapter headings (like Chapter 7: Going All the Way) to a style like Heading 1 using a program like Word or OpenOffice. For any subheadings (like Amazon Kindle) you want to use a different heading like Heading 3. This will create your table of contents for you, so there is no need to put one in the document itself. Add a page break at the end of each chapter. Save your document using the file type "Web Page, Filtered."

Search the Web for the program MobiPocket Creator (which the Amazon Kindle site links to directly) or the Calibre program if you have a Mac. Import your document (which is now an HTML file) and click on the Cover section to import your cover file. Click on Table of Contents and place "h1" in the top left box and "h3" in the middle left box. Click "Build" to build your book into a Kindle file.

Download the program Kindle Previewer and then import the file you created. Here you will be able to see if there are any formatting mistakes for your document. Change the errors in the original Word or OpenOffice document and then repeat the same procedure.

When you sign up for the Amazon Kindle publishing service, all you need to do is create a new book listing, upload your cover file, upload your book file and fill in information like the book description, price, etc.

I have simplified the process largely, but this is essentially all you have to do. Do not let tedious tasks like this slow you down, for the sooner you have the book online, the sooner you can call yourself an author.

## Amazon CreateSpace

I'll admit that my knowledge is a bit limited on CreateSpace as I'm just starting to work with it myself. The reason it got my attention in the first place is that unlike self-publishing programs like Lulu that create print versions of digital books, CreateSpace sells the books on Amazon. It gives people without a Kindle who see your Kindle book on Amazon another chance to purchase the book in print-form.

It helps to either have a bit of design experience or outsource the design of your book cover, since it includes the spine of the book and the back cover with CreateSpace. You also may need someone to design the inside of the book, to ensure that it looks professional when you have it printed. While it can be free to sign up for, I hear that the Pro Plan which costs $39 per book can be beneficial as it increases royalties and decreases the cost per book for authors.

A similar platform to CreateSpace, called Lightning Source may be worth a try. While it does not sell to the main Amazon site, it apparently sells the book more in international markets than CreateSpace does. If you're interested in getting the book out to the world at large, this might be a good option for you.

## Smashwords

Smashwords is a powerful e-book publishing website that distributes books to Barnes & Noble, Sony, Apple, Kobo, Diesel, and to its own growing library. While the site takes the longest to pay royalties (since it's waiting for all the distributors to pay them before they can pay you) it's very cool to see your book in so many different places. I recently found out that you can now submit to Barnes & Noble directly through their Pub It! program as well.

Smashwords is a different format entirely than Kindle and their process requires no page breaks and no additional lines in between paragraphs, chapters, etc. There are other things to keep in mind like their table of contents and formatting for special books like plays. The site has the most extensive guide to document forming I've seen and a few glances through it will do more justice to the process than I can do here.

Once you submit the book in a Word (or OpenOffice) document, Smashwords takes on the cool task of converting your book into every possible format for all the different vendors. Since the site lets you download a complimentary version of each format, this is helpful if you want to give a friend with an eReader a copy of your book but you aren't sure how to convert it yourself.

I didn't see much in the way of results from Smashwords at first, but when I checked back after a couple of months, I was astonished to find that I'd sold books on Kindle, Apple, Smashwords, Sony and Barnes & Noble. I'm interested to see how the site does for me once an entire year has passed by.

## E-Junkie

E-Junkie is a website that can host your documents so that a simple link will allow them to purchase the product directly from your website. For this process, you will need a money managing site like PayPal to deal with the transactions. I have used some simple PDF creating programs like Adobe Acrobat to turn my books into a file with a table of contents that would be easy for people to read on their computers. After uploading the file and giving E-Junkie my PayPal information, it's as easy as posting the links on my site.

For uploading a couple of books, the site does cost $5 a month, but it offers security and it saves you having to host the book on your own site. You get to set your own price and you get a higher cut than you would if someone bought your book off of the Kindle or Smashwords website. If your website gets a ton of traffic, this can be a very effective sales method.

If you plan on pricing your book below $12 (most of mine retail for $2.99 as an eBook), it would be smart for you to sign up for PayPal Micropayments. Joining this free service of PayPal makes sure that when you sell cheaper items, they take a lower per transaction cut. This saved me between five and 10 cents per transaction, which over time can definitely add up.

## Conclusion

I don't give you all of these options so much as a choice of one over another. I personally feel as though it's best to submit your book to all of them. I have heard stories of people finding great success on Kindle; I've heard of those with no success on Kindle but with major success on Nook (Pub It!); I've even heard of those who had no success on the digital sites but who had a blast making sales on CreateSpace. There is no telling which site your book will sell on the most effectively. Try them all, do some promotion like advertising and posting on sites like Shelfari, Twitter, Kindleboards and others, and see what happens. You may go from Average Joe to Amazon Selling Author in just a few short months after digital publishing.

# 8 THE NEXT STEP

When I published my first book and as I waited and hoped that it would sell, I was sort of at a loss for what to do next. Did I want to wait and see if it was successful before I kept writing? Should I try to launch right into the next story I can think of? Should I promote this book for the conceivable future until it's successful?

While I think there's no right way or wrong way with your decision, I personally feel as though you should devote a little time to promotion and you should start working on the next book. There's nothing better to keep you motivated than a new goal, a new challenge. If you determined that your purpose was something like "I want to tell entertaining stories to the world," remind yourself that you said "stories" and not just one story.

Another thing to keep in mind is that even though you've self-published your first book and even if it sells relatively well, it doesn't mean that you've "made it" and that you should quit your job right away. Unless you're selling 10,000 copies of the book each month, you should probably keep the "writer on the side" position until you hit that mark or higher.

If this book has caused you to gain any positive habits, do not stop them once you've finished your book. Keep them going and continue to take down notes and eat healthily and prepare for your next great idea. If you don't have one yet, just keep it up and be ready for it to strike at any moment.

The one thing I really do know about your next step is that self-publishing through a digital method is truly like the Wild West right now. It's an undiscovered country for many authors and more and more writers are starting to warm up to it every single day. It's an amazing time for a writer on the side, because you don't need to make lengthy book proposals to publishers, you just write, edit, design and publish. E-Books are going to be around for a long time and I'm proud to be a part of this strange and unusual world.

Good luck out there in the world of writing. Feel free to drop me a line anytime at my Build Creative Writing Ideas site. Until then, happy writing!

# ABOUT THE AUTHOR

Bryan Cohen has spent the last few years writing articles and books to help people become motivated to write from his Build Creative Writing Ideas website. He has also dabbled in theatre, film and promotional sales work during his time in the chilly city of Chicago. He graduated with degrees in English and Dramatic Art with a minor in Creative Writing from the University of North Carolina at Chapel Hill in 2005. He has produced several plays he has written or co-written including *Chekhov Kegstand, Covenant Coffee, Something from Nothing, Kerpow!* and *The Morning After.* His books include *1,000 Creative Writing Prompts: Ideas for Blogs, Scripts, Stories and More, Sharpening the Pencil: Essays on Writing, Motivation and Enjoying Your Life,* and *500 Writing Prompts for Kids: First Grade through Fifth Grade.* He currently lives in Chicago just a block away from historic Wrigley Field.

Visit his website at http://www.build-creative-writing-ideas.com